上海体育博物馆

Shanghai Sports
Museum

上海体育博物馆珍品典藏

Treasure Collection of Shanghai Sports Museum

Edited by
Shanghai Sports Publicity and Education Center
上海市体育宣传教育中心 / 编

Shanghai Scientific & Technical Publishers
上海科学技术出版社

编辑委员会

EDITORIAL BOARD

上海
体育博物馆
珍品典藏

前言
FOREWORD

前言

FOREWORD

1843 年，上海开埠后，西方近代体育文化传入上海，上海本土文化在与其交融吸纳重建的过程中，形成了特有的近代上海体育文化。上海由此开创了中国近代体育的多个第一。从 1851 年举办中国第一次骑马竞赛到 2014 年环球马术冠军赛登陆上海；从 1852 年在黄浦江举办中国第一次划船比赛到 2021 年首届上海赛艇公开赛在苏州河举行；从 1890 年中国第一个以田径为主的运动会在圣约翰书院举办到 2005 年国际田联钻石联赛落户上海；从 1904 年乒乓球运动传入上海到徐寅生、王励勤等上海乒乓球运动员人才辈出；从 1932 年中国奥运第一人刘长春从上海新关码头远赴洛杉矶出征第十届夏季奥运会到 2021 年上海共培养出 17 位奥运冠军……上海体育在历史进程中开拓创新、历久弥新，从中孕育出独一无二的体育珍品，传递着上海体育的无限魅力。

2021 年 7 月 11 日，上海体育博物馆建成并向社会免费开放。博物馆坐落于南京西路150号体育大厦内，其原址为建成于1928年的西侨青年会大楼。这是一座以“传承体育文化，弘扬体育精神”为宗旨的综合性体育博物馆。经过一年的开放运行，这里已经成为具有海派文化特色的市民公共体育文化空间和城市体育文化坐标。

馆内设有“历史之舟”“奥运之光”“活力之城”“未来之窗”四个展厅，共展出珍贵藏品2 000余件，生动地展现了上海体育的历史和发展历程。本书甄选了119套375件博物馆藏品，向公众讲述上海体育的历史文化和藏品背后鲜为人知的故事，是研究上海体育史中不可或缺的文化印记。让更多的人了解上海体育，感受上海体育独有的魅力，为上海建设全球著名体育城市增添动力。

After Shanghai's opening as a treaty port in 1843, modern western sports culture was introduced into Shanghai. In the process of blending, absorbing and rebuilding with Shanghai local culture, a unique modern Shanghai sports culture was formed. Shanghai has thus created a number of first in modern Chinese sports. From hosting China's first race meeting in 1851 to the arrival of the Global Equestrian Championship in Shanghai in 2014; from hosting China's first rowing competition on the Huangpu River in 1852 to the first Shanghai Open Rowing on the Suzhou River in 2021. From 1890, when China's first athletics-based games were held at St. John's College, to 2005, when the IAAF Diamond League landed in Shanghai; from 1904, when table tennis was introduced to Shanghai, to the emergence of Shanghai table tennis players such as Xu Yinsheng and Wang Liqin; from 1932, when Liu Changchun, the first Chinese Olympian, travelled from Shanghai Xinguan Wharf to Los Angeles to compete in the 10th Summer Olympics, to 2021, a total of 17 Olympic Champions have been produced in Shanghai...Shanghai sports has pioneered and innovated in the historical process, and its history has been renewed. Sports treasures conveying the infinite charm of Shanghai sports.

On July 11, 2021, the Shanghai Sports Museum was completed and opened to the public free of charge. The museum is located in the Sports Building, No.150 West Nanjing Road. Its original site was Foreign YMCA Building, which was built in 1928. This is a comprehensive sports museum with the purpose for " inheriting sports culture and promoting sports spirit". After one year of opening, it has become a public sports cultural space for citizens and a coordinate of urban sports culture with Shanghai style cultural characteristics.

There are four exhibition halls in the museum. "A Retrospect of the History" "Olympic Glory of Shanghai" "A city

Full of Vitality" and "A Window of the Future", with more than 2,000 treasure collections on display, vividly showing the history and development of Shanghai sports. This book selects 119 sets of 375 museum collections to tell the public about the history and culture of Shanghai sports and the little-known stories behind the collections. It is an indispensable cultural imprint in the study of Shanghai sports history. Let more people know about Shanghai sports, feel the unique charm of Shanghai sports, and add impetus for Shanghai to build a world-renowned sports city.

目录

CONTENTS

Treasure
Collection
of
Shanghai
Sports
Museum

序厅

LOBBY

绪论

INTRODUCTION

序厅

LOBBY

第二十九届夏季奥运会运动项目瓷雕

Porcelain Sculptures of Various Sports at the 29th Summer Olympics

□ With the world patent "chamfering and demoulding method", the porcelain breaks through the limitation of traditional modeling. In the smooth lines of the new Western art, it perfectly integrates the elegant humanistic temperament of the East, converts the sensation of the scenes of Olympic competition into eternal beauty, shows the movements and beauty of athletes, and keeps the spirit of the Olympic on the porcelain. Each piece of work is made of high-grade porcelain soil,which has been carefully made through manual work and hundreds of working procedures. Each work is provided with a certificate and is numbered. This set of 29 porcelain works represents the 29th Olympic Games.

□ 瓷器制作工艺为世界专利的"倒角脱模法"，突破传统造型限制，在西方新艺术的流畅线条中，完美融入东方典雅的人文气质，将奥运竞技场刹那间之感动化为永恒之美，表现出运动员之律动与美感，将奥运精神常驻瓷品之上。每件作品皆采用高级细致瓷土，经过纯手工及上百道工序，精心制作完成。每件都配有证书，均有编号。该套瓷器 29 件，寓意着第 29 届奥运会。

垒球项目
Softball
尺寸 /Size:
216mm × 127mm × 305mm
重量 /Weight:
779.1g
年代 /Date:
2008

足球项目
Football
尺寸 /Size:
241mm × 121mm × 298mm
重量 /Weight
1 000.3g

羽毛球项目
Badminton
尺寸 /Size：
121mm × 102mm × 333mm
重量 /Weight：
532.2g

游泳项目
Swimming
尺寸 /Size：
267mm × 108mm × 229mm
重量 /Weight：
1 230.8g

棒球项目
Baseball
尺寸 /Size：
229mm × 108mm × 318mm
重量 /Weight：
819.5g

艺术体操项目
Rhythmic Gymnastics
尺寸 /Size:
140mm × 95mm × 276mm
重量 /Weight:
809.2g

跳水项目
Diving
尺寸 /Size:
178mm × 114mm × 387mm
重量 /Weight:
952.5g

网球项目
Tennis
尺寸 /Size:
146mm × 121mm × 305mm
重量 /Weight:
793.2g

摔跤项目
Wrestling
尺寸 /Size:
178mm × 165mm × 314mm
重量 /Weight:
901.6g

田径项目
Athletics
尺寸 /Size:
181mm × 159mm × 324mm
重量 /Weight:
1 314.2g

跆拳道项目
Taekwondo
尺寸 /Size:
180mm × 150mm × 320mm
重量 /Weight:
1 133.4g

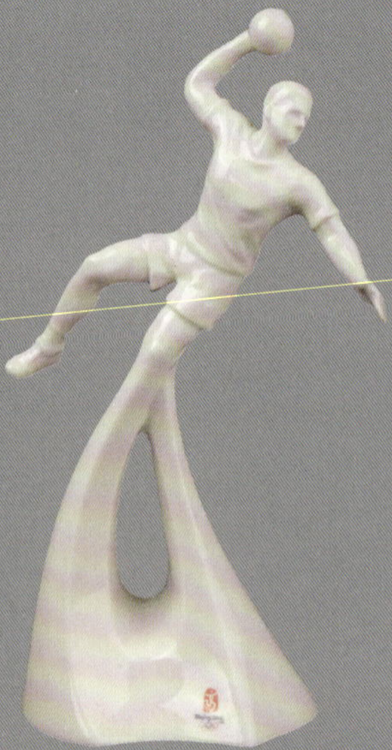

手球项目
Handball
尺寸 /Size:
181mm × 108mm × 324mm
重量 /Weight:
513.8g

射击项目
Shooting
尺寸 /Size:
191mm × 159mm × 318mm
重量 /Weight:
1 020.5g

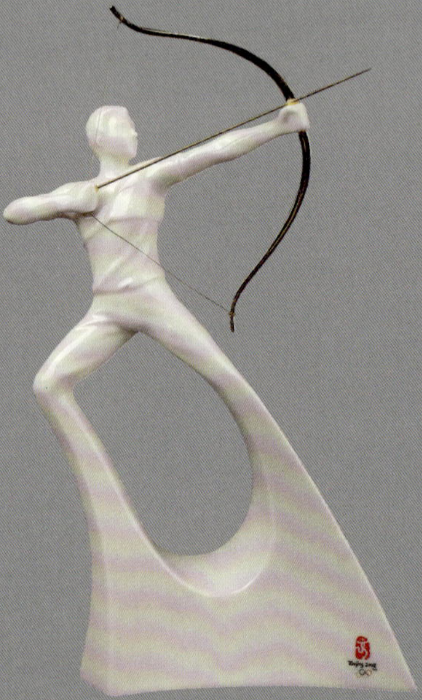

射箭项目
Archery
尺寸 /Size:
206mm × 86mm × 337mm
重量 /Weight:
637.2g

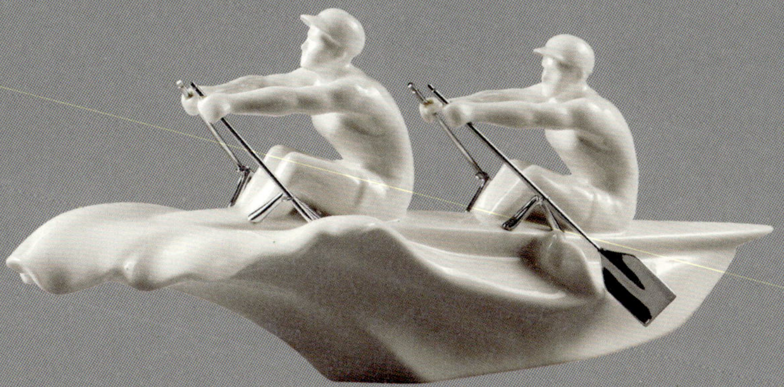

赛艇项目
Rowing
尺寸 /Size:
400mm × 110mm × 170mm
重量 /Weight:
1 224.7g

赛跑项目
Race
尺寸 /Size:
360mm × 140mm × 220mm
重量 /Weight:
1 079.8g

沙滩排球项目
Beach Volleyball
尺寸 /Size:
175mm × 127mm × 343mm
重量 /Weight:
841.2g

乒乓球项目
Table Tennis
尺寸 /Size:
216mm × 121mm × 282mm
重量 /Weight:
971.2g

曲棍球项目
Hockey
尺寸 /Size:
310mm × 90mm × 320mm
重量 /Weight:
1 105.4g

篮球项目
Basketball
尺寸 /Size:
162mm × 133mm × 403mm
重量 /Weight:
1 037g

举重项目
Weightlifting
尺寸 /Size:
216mm × 171mm × 305mm
重量 /Weight:
689.2g

击剑项目
Fencing
尺寸 /Size:
305mm × 95mm × 273mm
重量 /Weight:
606.1g

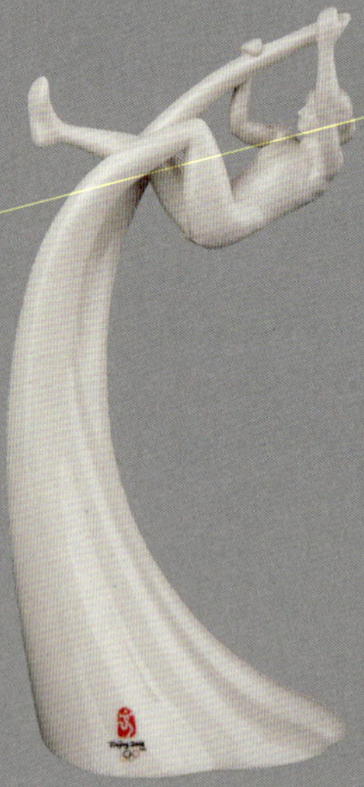

撑杆跳项目
Pole Vault
尺寸 /Size:
165mm × 108mm × 330mm
重量 /Weight:
841g

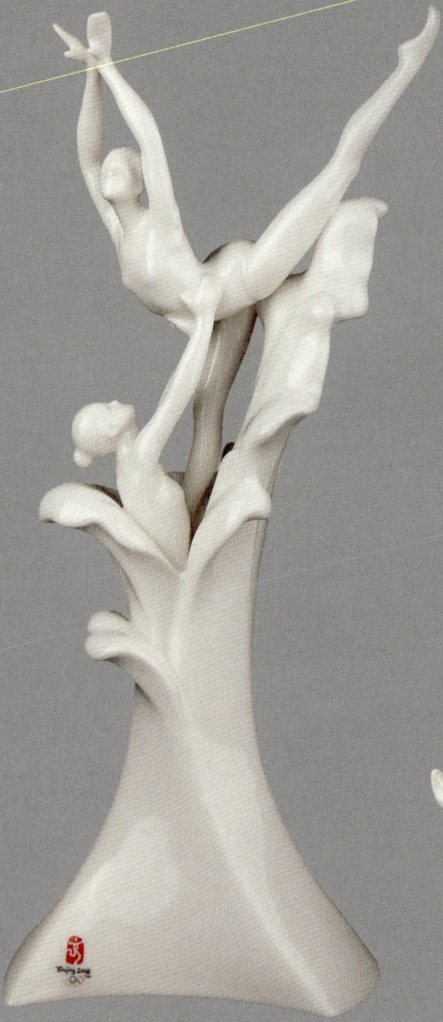

花样游泳项目
Synchronized Swimming
尺寸 /Size:
165mm × 108mm × 403mm
重量 /Weight:
1 027g

马术项目
Equestrian
尺寸 /Size:
229mm × 156mm × 330mm
重量 /Weight:
995.9g

鞍马项目
Pommel Horse
尺寸 /Size：
181mm × 95mm × 295mm
重量 /Weight：
514.1g

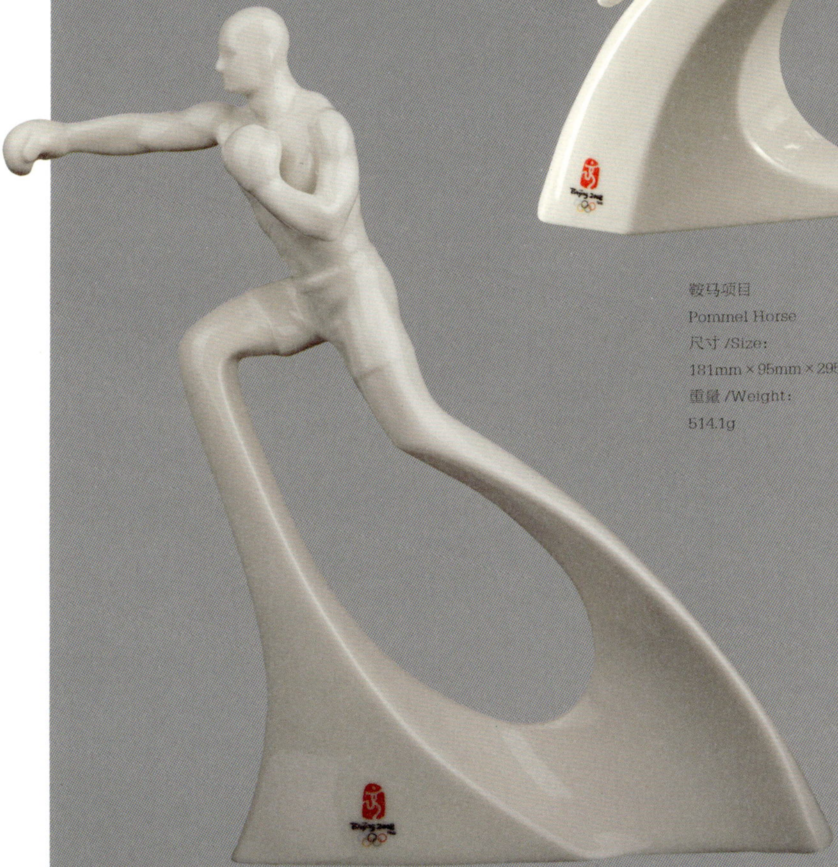

拳击项目
Boxing
尺寸 /Size：
260mm × 92mm × 267mm
重量 /Weight：
692.2g

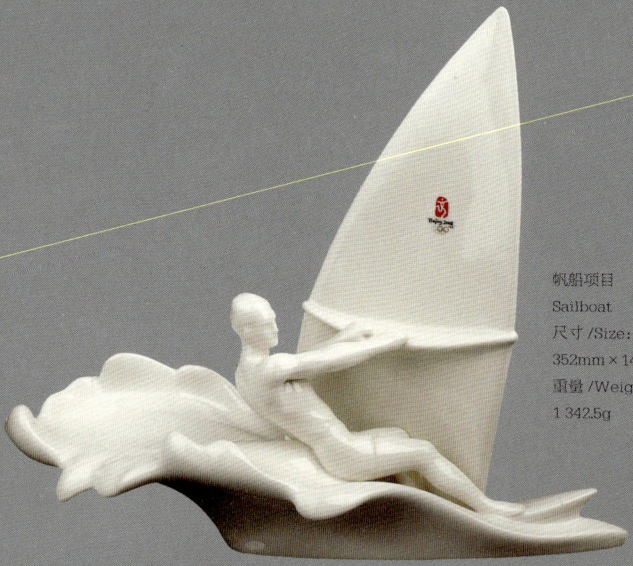

帆船项目
Sailboat
尺寸 /Size:
352mm × 143mm × 295mm
重量 /Weight:
1 342.5g

皮划艇项目
Canoe
尺寸 /Size:
286mm × 108mm × 184mm
重量 /Weight:
978.4g

第一展厅

EXHIBITION HALL I

历史

A RETROSPECT

之舟

OF THE HISTORY

第一展厅

EXHIBITION HALL I

1843 年
（道光二十三年），
上海开埠，
西方近代体育文化随着
侨民一起登陆上海滩。
初期的近代体育活动只在租界内
的侨民间流行，
直到 20 世纪 20 年代，
才开始接纳华人。
由最初的惊诧、排斥，
到调和、吸纳，
近代体育完成了本土化的嬗变，
并开始向周边辐射。
上海，
成为西方体育传入中国的
主要扩散地和
中国近代体育的
发源地之一。

After Shanghai's opening
as a treaty port in 1843,
the 23rd year
during the reign of Daoguang Emperor
of Qing Dynasty,
modern Western sports culture came
to Shanghai along with the foreign nationals.
At first,
modern sports activities were only
popular among foreign nationals
in the concessions,
and it was not until the 1920s
that some venues began to open to the Chinese.
The attitude towards sports
of the Chinese people gradually changed
from surprise
and rejection at the beginning to
later reconciliation
and acceptance.
Modern sports then completed
its localization and began to spread
to surrounding areas,
and naturally,
Shanghai became a major city
for the introduction of Western sports into
and its spread in China and
one of the cradles
of modern Chinese sports.

HANDBALL
CYCLING ROAD
ARCHERY

李森

Pony No.
1 MW
5th Race

上海跑马主题展品

Exhibition of Shanghai Racing Meeting Theme

道光三十年（1850），侨民霍格（W. HOGG）、吉勃（T. D. GIBB）、兰雷（LANGLEY）、派金（W. W. PAKIN）、韦勃（E. WEBB）5人组织跑马总会（SHANGHAI RACE CLUB），自任董事，建成第一个赛马场（老公园），于第二年进行了第一次赛马。咸丰四年（1854），把南京路、河南路口的老公园分10块以每亩超过200两银子的价格卖出。又从浙江中路南京路两侧以9 700两银子的代价圈定了第二个跑马场（新公园）。咸丰十一年（1861）又以100 036两银子的价格卖掉第二个跑马场，在今人民公园处强圈了500亩地建成第三个跑马场和跑马厅（现上海市历史博物馆、上海革命历史博物馆），成立跑马总会。跑马总会实行董事制，由7人组成董事会，董事由每年召开的跑马总会基本会员大会选举产生，设董事长1人。每届董事都以英国侨民为主，董事会下设书记，是专职管理人员。总会下设两大部门，一是俱乐部，设在跑马厅内，有滚球室、弹子房、餐厅、酒吧、打牌间等设施。每处都有干事管理。二为跑马场，内设顾问、执事、监守等职务，多数由总会会员担任。

跑马总会会员有正式会员和其他会员之分，除华人外，外国人均可申请为正式会员，但申请后需投票委员会表决。光绪三十四年（1908）以后，曾吸收了少量华人为名誉会员、聘请会员或社会会员，当时共有正式会员320人，其他会员500人，两种会员权利差异较多，非正式会员只能在节日参加赛马，但交纳会费则两种会员相同，均为每月10元。赛马活动于同治二年（1863）至1919年之间每年举行两次。春季赛马于4月下旬至5月上旬；秋季赛马于10月下旬至11月中旬，每次都进行3天。1920年后增加了几天预赛，有时也在周末或节日举行赛马。

跑马总会组织赛马只进行组织工作，并不供应马匹，参赛马匹均由马主私人豢养。跑马总会的收入除门票以外，主要靠赛马时博彩抽成，宣统元年（1909）以前，采用挂牌定额分彩的方式，由各赌摊的老板向跑马厅交纳保证金后在场内设摊开赌，盈亏由摊主负责，跑马厅坐收盈利。以后为了追求更多利润，在赛马之前发行各种彩票，其中以香槟票为最多，华人买此彩票者甚多。据1920年至1939年统计，香槟票、独赢票两种彩票的收入就达14 139万多元，合计每年700多万元。到抗日战争全面爆发前夕，跑马总会尚积余2 000多万元。20世纪二三十年代，是跑马总会的全盛时代，跑马总会成了整个跑马厅所有场地的真正主人。

In the thirty Years of Daoguang (1850), five nationals, namely, W.Hogg, T.D.Gibb, Langley, W.W.Pakin and E.Webb organized the Shanghai Race Club, serving as a director, and built the first racecourse (old park). They carried out the first horse race in the second year. In the fourth year of Xianfeng (1854), the old park at the intersection of Nanjing Road and Henan Road was sold at a price of more than 200 silver dollars per mu in 10 blocks. The second racecourse (new park) was delineated from both sides of Nanjing Road, Central Zhejiang Road at the cost of 9,700 silver dollars. In the 11th year of Xianfeng (1861), the second racecourse was sold at the price of 100,036 silver dollars. At present, the third racecourse Now Shanghai History Museum, Shanghai Revolutionary History Museum with an area of 500 mu was surrounded in the People's Park. Shanghai Race Club implements director system, consisting of 7 members of the board of directors, and the directors shall be elected by the annual general meeting of the basic members of the club, with one chairman. Each director is dominated by British nationals, and the secretary under the Board of Directors is full-time management personnel. There are two departments under the Shanghai Race Club, One is the club, which is located upstairs from the bleaching hall. It has petanque rooms, billiard rooms, restaurants, bars, and card rooms. Every room is managed by an officer. The other is a racecourse, with consultants, executives, supervisors and other positions, most of which are held by members of the Club.

The members of the Shanghai Race Club are divided into formal members and other members. Except for ethnic Chinese, foreigners can apply for formal members, but the voting committee must vote after application. After the 34th year of the reign of Emperor Guangxu (1908), a small number of Chinese were absorbed as honorary, hired or social members. At that time, there were 320 formal members and 500 other members. There were many differences in the rights of the two members. Informal members could only participate in the horse racing at festivals, but the membership fees were the same for both members, which were 10 yuan per month. Horse racing dates are held twice a year between the 2nd year of the reign of Emperor Tongzhi (1863) and 1919. The horse racing in spring lasts from late April to early May; the horse racing in autumn lasts from late October to mid-November for 3 days each time. After 1920, several days of pre-competitions were added, and sometimes horse racing was held on weekends or festivals.

Shanghai Race Club is only responsible for the organization of horse races and does not supply horses. Horses participating in the competition are maintained by horse owners. In addition to the tickets, the revenue of the Club mainly depends on the commission of the gambling of horse racing. Before the 1st year of the reign of Emperor Xuantong (1909), the method of the fixed quota of gambling is adopted. The owners of each gambling booth pay the deposit to the racecourse and then they will spread the gambling. The profit and loss will be borne by the vendor, and the racecourse will be profitable. In the future, in order to pursue more profits, various raffle tickets were issued before the horse races, among which champagne tickets were the most, and many Chinese bought this raffle ticket. Between 1920 to 1939, the two raffles, champagne and Solo, general revenues of over 141.39 million yuan, a combined total of over 7 million yuan per year. On the eve of the War of Resistance Against Japanese Aggression, the Race Club still had a surplus of more than 20 million yuan. During the 1920s and 1930s, were the heyday of the Race Club, which became the real owner of all the venues in the entire Race Club.

上海赛马会丝质赛程公告

Shanghai Race Club Competition Schedule out of silk

The Shanghai Horse Racing Conference announced the tournament on April 26 and 27, 1866. The competitions on each day are divided into many competitions, such as the Challenger Cup, Home Cup, Yangtze Cup and Hong Kong Cup, attracting dozens of horses to participate. The announcement details the height, weight, name and other information of all horses, and also distinguishes the horses by breed.

上海赛马会于1866年4月26日及27日的赛程公告，各日比赛分为挑战者杯、家园杯、扬子杯和香港杯等多项比赛，吸引数十匹赛马参赛。公告详细记录了全部赛马的身高、体重和名称等信息，也有按马种将马加以区分。

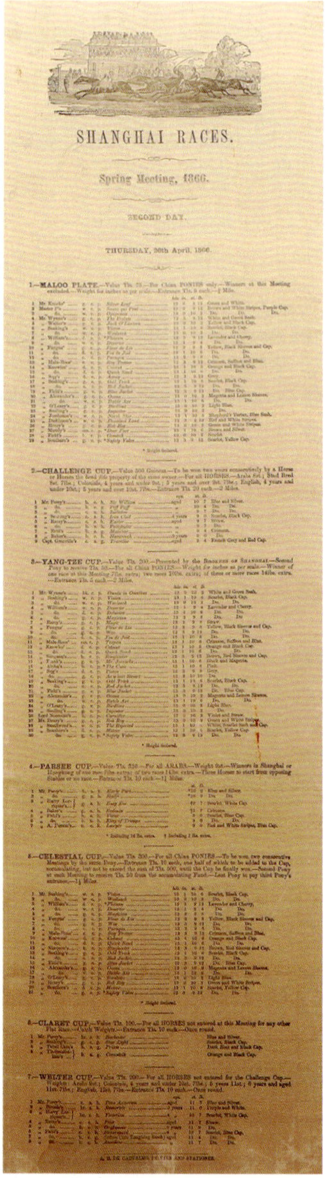
SHANGHAI RACES.

Spring Meeting, 1866.

SECOND DAY.

THURSDAY, 26th April, 1866.

尺寸 /Size:
660mm × 180mm
790mm × 200mm
年代 /Date:
1866

SHANGHAI RACES.

Spring Meeting, 1866.

THIRD DAY.

FRIDAY, 27th April, 1866.

1.—CHAASEE CUP.—Value Tls. 300.—For China and Japan PONIES.—Weight for inches as per scale.—Winners of two or more races at this Meeting 10lbs. extra; of one race 7lbs. extra.—Entrance Tls. 10 each.—1 Mile.

No.	Owner				Pony	hds.	in.	st.	lb.	Colours
1	Mr. Knook's	g.	c.	p.	*Silver Leaf*	12	3	9	12	Green and White.
2	Master P.'s	w.	c.	p.	*Sauve qui Peut*	12	3	9	12	Brown and White Stripes, Purple Cap.
3	do.	w.	c.	p.	*Oppressor*	13	0	10	2	Do. Do. Do.
4	Mr. Seaking's	w.	c.	p.	*Vision*	13	1	10	6	Scarlet, Black Cap.
5	,, do.	w.	c.	p.	*Woolsack*	13	0	10	2	Do. Do.
6	,, William's	d.	c.	p.	*Flotsam*	12	3	9	12	Lavender and Cherry.
7	,, do.	w.	c.	p.	*Deserter*	12	1	9	4	Do. Do.
8	,, do.	w.	c.	p.	*Ambition*	13	1	10	6	Do. Do.
9	,, Fungus'	g.	c.	p.	*Fleur de Lis*	12	2	9	8	Yellow, Black Sleeves and Cap.
10	,, do.	g.	c.	p.	*Wee*	12	3	9	12	Do. Do.
11	,, do.	c.	c.	p.	*Paragon*	12	2	9	8	Do. Do.
12	,, do.	d.	c.	p.	*Feu de Joie*	13	1	10	6	Do. Do.
13	,, Male-Ross'	cm.	c.	p.	*Tinpan*	13	1	10	6	Crimson, Saffron and Blue.
14	,, Knowles'	d.	c.	p.	*Colonel*	13	1	10	6	Orange and Black Cap.
15	,, do.	d.	c.	p.	*Quick Sand*	13	1	10	6	Do. Do.
16	,, Sigg's	d.	c.	p.	*Agony*	12	3	9	12	Grey.
17	,, Seaking's	g.	c.	p.	*Odd Trick*	13	1	10	6	Scarlet, Black Cap.
18	,, do.	c.	c.	p.	*Red Jacket*	12	3	9	12	Do. Do.
19	,, Field's	g.	c.	p.	*Blue Jacket*	12	3	9	12	Do. Blue Cap.
20	,, Alexander's	g.	c.	p.	*Ozone*	13	0	10	2	Magenta and Lemon Sleeves.
21	,, do.	w.	c.	p.	*Battle Axe*	13	1	10	6	Do. Do.
22	,, O'Leary's	g.	c.	p.	*Birdlime*	13	0	10	2	Light Blue.
23	Lord Nonsense's	b.	c.	p.	*Carnifex*	13	0	10	2	Violet and Straw.
24	Mr. Henry's	g.	c.	p.	*Rob Roy*	13	0	10	2	Green and White Stripes.
25	,, Southern's	g.	c.	p.	*Europe*	12	3	9	12	Scarlet, Yellow Cap.
26	,, do.	g.	c.	p.	**Safety Valve*	12	3	9	12	Do. Do.

* Height declared.

2.—COLONIAL SWEEPSTAKES.—A Sweepstakes of Tls. 25 each, with Tls. 200 added.—For all Colonial HORSES; to be Handicapped by the Stewards at the end of the second day's races.—Entrance Tls. 10 each.—2 Miles.

No.	Owner				Horse	age.	st.	lb.	Colours
1	Mr. Perry's	c.	s.	h.	*Jacholes*				Blue and Silver.
2	,, do.	c.	s.	h.	*Pons Asinorum*				Do. Do.
3	,, Rennie's	br.	s.	h.	*Ramornie*				Purple and White.
4	,, Harry Lee-tipper's	b.	c.	h.	*Veronica*				Scarlet, White Cap.
5	,, Seaking's	c.	s.	h.	*Iron Clad*				Do. Black Cap.
6	,, Barry's	c.	s.	h.	*Exeter*				Straw.
7	,, do.	b.	s.	h.	*Pathfinder*				Do.
8	,, Reid's	b.	s.	g.	*Malabar*				Crimson.
9	,, Field's	c.	s.	h.	*Beauregard*				Scarlet, Blue Cap.
10	,, do.	b.	s.	g.	*Stilton (late Laughing Stock)*				Do. Do.
11	,, do.	b.	c.	h.	*Anecdote*				Do. Do.
12	Capt. Grenville's	c.	s.	g.	*Traveller*				French Grey and Red Cap.

3.—SELLING STAKES.—For China PONIES.—If Entered at a Value of Tls. 600, to carry 11st. 7lbs.; under that amount to be Handicapped by the Stewards according to the Value at which Entered.—The owner of the second Pony may claim the Winner; otherwise the winner to be sold immediately after the race, at Auction, with all his Engagements.—Any amount realised by such sale, over and above the sum at which the Pony has been Entered, to go to the Fund.—Entrance Tls. 5 each, with Tls. 100 added from the Fund.—2 Miles.

Owner				Pony	st.	lb.	Value	Colours
Mr. Wynne's	bk.	c.	p.	*Omnia in Omnibus*	10	7	Tls. 200.	White and Green Sash.
,, Seaking's	w.	c.	p.	*Vision*	10	3	,, 150.	Scarlet, Black Cap.
,, do.	w.	c.	p.	*Woolsack*	10	0	,, 100.	Do. Do.
,, William's	w.	c.	p.	*Deserter*	9	10	,, 50.	Lavender and Cherry.
,, do.	d.	c.	p.	*Delusion*	10	0	,, 100.	Do. Do.
,, do.	d.	c.	p.	**Flotsam*	10	0	,, 100.	Do. Do.
,, Barry's	g.	c.	p.	*Magic*	10	7	,, 200.	Straw.
,, Fungus'	d.	c.	p.	*Feu de Joie*	10	3	,, 150.	Yellow, Black Sleeves & Cap.
,, do.	c.	c.	p.	*Paragon*	10	7	,, 200.	Do. Do.
,, do.	g.	c.	p.	*Wee*	10	7	,, 200.	Do. Do.
,, do.	g.	c.	p.	*Constable*	10	0	,, 100.	Do. Do.
,, Male-Ross'	c.	c.	p.	*Boy Trotter*	10	0	,, 100.	Crimson, Saffron and Blue.
,, do.	cm.	c.	p.	*Tinpan*	9	10	,, 50.	Do. Do.
,, Simpson's	b.	c.	p.	*Ringleader*	10	7	,, 200.	Brown, Red Sleeves and Cap.
,, Frank's	g.	c.	p.	*Mr. Jorrocks*	10	10	,, 250.	Black and Magenta.
,, Alpha's	c.	c.	p.	*Spring Jack*	10	7	,, 200.	Pink.
,, Sigg's	d.	c.	p.	*Plover*	9	10	,, 85.	Grey.
,, do.	d.	c.	p.	*As a last Resort*	9	12	,, 75.	Do.
,, Seaking's	g.	c.	p.	*Odd Trick*	10	0	,, 100.	Scarlet, Black Cap.
,, do.	c.	c.	p.	*Red Jacket*	10	0	,, 100.	Do. Do.
,, Field's	g.	c.	p.	*Blue Jacket*	10	0	,, 100.	Do. Blue Cap.
,, Alexander's	g.	c.	p.	*Ozone*	10	10	,, 250.	Magenta and Lemon Sleeves.
,, do.	w.	c.	p.	*Battle Axe*	10	10	,, 250.	Do. Do.
,, do.	d.	c.	p.	*Tornado*	10	0	,, 100.	Do. Do.
,, do.	g.	c.	p.	*Cyclone*	10	0	,, 100.	Do. Do.
,, O'Leary's	g.	c.	p.	*Birdlime*	11	7	,, 400.	Light Blue.
,, Snelling's	g.	c.	p.	*Impostor*	9	10	,, 50.	Do.
,, Samuel's	g.	c.	p.	*Monogram*	9	10	,, 50.	Do.
,, Henry's	g.	c.	p.	*Rob Roy*	11	0	,, 300.	Green and White Stripes.
,, Manly's	cm.	c.	p.	**Deer Foot*	10	3	,, 150.	Brown and Silver.
,, Southern's	d.	c.	p.	*Meteor*	10	0	,, 100.	Scarlet, Yellow Cap.
,, do.	g.	c.	p.	**Safety Valve*	9	8	,, 25.	Do. Do.
,, Field's	b.	c.	p.	*Cossack*	9	8	,, 25.	Scarlet.

* Height declared.

4.—HOME CUP.—Value 100 Guineas—Presented by a Subscriber.—For all HORSES.—Arabs 8st. 7lbs.; Colonials, 4 years and under 9st. 6lbs.; 5 years 9st. 12lbs.; 6 years and aged 10st. 4lbs.;—English, 4 years and under 10st. 8lbs.; 5 years 10st. 10lbs.; 6 years and aged 11st.—Entrance Tls. 10 each.—1½ Miles.

Owner				Horse	age.	st.	lb.	Colours
Mr. Perry's	b.	a.	h.	*Sir William*	aged	*11	0	Blue and Silver.
,, do.	b.	a.	g.	*Puff Puff*	,,	10	11	Do. Do.
,, do.	c.	s.	h.	*Jacholes*	,,	10	4	Do. Do.
,, do.	c.	s.	h.	*Pons Asinorum*	,,	10	4	Do. Do.
,, Rennie's	br.	s.	h.	*Ramornie*	5 years	9	12	Purple and White.
,, Barry's	c.	s.	h.	*Exeter*	aged	10	4	Straw.
,, do.	b.	s.	h.	*Pathfinder*	,,	10	4	Do.
,, Baker's	b.	c.	h.	*Hunnasah*	3 years	9	4	Crimson.
Capt. Grenville's	c.	s.	g.	*Traveller*	aged	10	1	French Grey and Scarlet Cap.

5.—CONSOLATION CUP.—Value Tls. 100.—For all beaten PONIES at this Meeting.—Weight for inches as per scale.—Entrance Tls. 5 each.—Once round.

Owner				Pony	hds.	in.	st.	lb.	Colours
Mr. Knook's	g.	c.	p.	*Silver Leaf*	12	3	9	12	Green and White.
Master P.'s	w.	c.	p.	*Sauve qui Peut*	12	3	9	12	Brown and White Stripes, Purple Cap.
,, do.	w.	c.	p.	*Oppressor*	13	0	10	2	Do. Do. Do.
Mr. Wynne's	g.	c.	p.	*The Prelate*	12	3	9	12	White and Green Sash.
,, do.	bk.	c.	p.	*Omnia in Omnibus*	13	0	10	2	Do. Do.
,, Waite's	c.	c.	p.	*Jack O'Lantern*	13	0	10	2	Yellow and Black Cap.
,, Seaking's	w.	c.	p.	*Vision*	13	1	10	6	Scarlet, Black Cap.
,, do.	w.	c.	p.	*Woolsack*	13	0	10	2	Do. Do.
,, William's	g.	c.	p.	*Magician*	12	2	9	8	Lavender and Cherry.
,, do.	d.	c.	p.	**Flotsam*	12	3	9	12	Do. Do.
,, do.	w.	c.	p.	*Deserter*	12	1	9	4	Do. Do.
,, Barry's	g.	c.	p.	*Magic*	12	2	9	8	Straw.
,, Fungus'	g.	c.	p.	*Fleur de Lis*	12	2	9	8	Yellow, Black Sleeves and Cap.
,, do.	c.	c.	p.	*Paragon*	12	2	9	8	Do. Do.
,, do.	d.	c.	p.	*Feu de Joie*	13	1	10	6	Do. Do.
,, do.	g.	c.	p.	*Wee*	12	3	9	12	Do. Do.
,, Male-Ross'	c.	c.	p.	*Boy Trotter*	12	3	9	12	Crimson, Saffron and Blue.
,, do.	w.	c.	p.	*Mendicant*	12	2	9	8	Do. Do.
,, do.	cm.	c.	p.	*Tinpan*	13	1	10	6	Do. Do.
,, do.	g.	c.	p.	**Rowdy*	12	3	9	10	Do. Do.
,, Knowles'	d.	c.	p.	*Colonel*	13	1	10	6	Orange and Black Cap.
,, do.	d.	c.	p.	*Quick Sand*	13	1	10	6	Do. Do.
,, Simpson's	b.	c.	p.	*Ringleader*	12	3	9	12	Brown, Red Sleeves and Cap.
,, Frank's	g.	c.	p.	*Mr. Jorrocks*	13	1	10	6	Black and Magenta.
,, Alpha's	b.	c.	p.	**The Cast*	13	1	10	6	Pink.
,, Sigg's	g.	c.	p.	*As a last Resort*	13	2	10	10	Grey.
,, do.	d.	c.	p.	*Plover*	12	2	9	8	Do.
,, Seaking's	g.	c.	p.	*Odd Trick*	13	1	10	6	Scarlet, Black Cap.
,, do.	c.	c.	p.	*Red Jacket*	12	3	9	12	Do. Do.
,, Field's	g.	c.	p.	*Blue Jacket*	12	3	9	12	Do. Blue Cap.
,, Alexander's	g.	c.	p.	*Ozone*	13	0	10	2	Magenta and Lemon Sleeves.
,, do.	w.	c.	p.	*Battle Axe*	13	1	10	6	Do. Do.
,, do.	d.	c.	p.	*Tornado*	13	1	10	6	Do. Do.
,, O'Leary's	g.	c.	p.	*Birdlime*	13	0	10	2	Light Blue.
,, Snelling's	g.	c.	p.	*Impostor*	13	0	10	2	Do.
,, Samuel's	g.	c.	p.	*Monogram*	12	2	9	8	Do.
,, Jardine's	w.	c.	p.	*North Star*	13	1	10	6	Shepherd's Tartan, Blue Sash.
Lord Nonsense's	b.	c.	p.	*Carnifex*	13	0	10	2	Violet and Straw.
Mr. Henry's	g.	c.	p.	*Rob Roy*	13	0	10	2	Green and White Stripes.
,, Smallwood's	w.	c.	p.	*The Rejected*	13	1	10	6	White, Scarlet Sash and Cap.
,, Southern's	g.	c.	p.	**Safety Valve*	12	3	9	12	Scarlet, Yellow Cap.
,, do.	d.	c.	p.	*Meteor*	13	1	10	6	Do. Do.
,, Field's	b.	c.	p.	*Cossack*	13	0	10	2	Do. Do.

* Height declared.

6.—THE SPRING CUP.—Value Tls. 300.—For all HORSES that have not won at this Meeting.—"Challenge Cup" weights.—Entrance Tls. 10 each.—1 Mile.

Owner				Horse	age.	st.	lb.	Colours
Mr. Perry's	br.	a.	h.	*Sir William*	aged.	10	7	Blue and Silver.
,, do.	c.	s.	h.	*Jacholes*	,,	9	7	Do. Do.
,, do.	c.	s.	h.	*Pons Asinorum*	,,	9	7	Do. Do.
,, Rennie's	br.	s.	h.	*Ramornie*	5 years.	9	7	Purple and White.
,, Harry Lee-tipper's	br.	s.	h.	*Veronica*	4 ,,	9	0	Scarlet, White Cap.
,, Seaking's	c.	s.	h.	*Iron Clad*	4 ,,	9	0	Do. Black Cap.
,, Barry's	c.	s.	h.	*Exeter*	aged.	9	7	Straw.
,, do.	c.	s.	h.	*Pilot*	,,	9	7	Do.
,, do.	b.	c.	h.	*Pathfinder*	,,	9	7	Do.
,, do.	b.	s.	h.	*Confidence*	5 years.	9	7	Do.
,, Reid's	b.	s.	g.	*Malabar*	aged.	9	4	Crimson.
,, Baker's	b.	c.	h.	*Hunnasah*	3 years.	9	0	Do.
Capt. Grenville's	c.	s.	g.	*Traveller*	aged.	9	4	French Grey and Red Cap.
Mr. Field's	c.	s.	h.	*Beauregard*	4 years.	9	0	Scarlet, Blue Cap.
,, do.	b.	a.	g.	*Stilton (late Laughing Stock)*	aged.	9	4	Do. Do.
,, do.	b.	c.	h.	*Anecdote*	,,	9	7	Do. Do.

7.—THE HONGKONG CUP.—Value Tls. 300.—Presented by the Hongkong Community.—A Steeple Chase for all HORSES.—Weights: Arabs 9st.; Stud Bred 10st.; Colonials 11st.; English 12st.—Entrance Tls. 10 each.—About 3 Miles.

Owner				Horse	age.	st.	lb.	Colours
Mr. Edward's	b.	a.	m.	*Lance*		11	11	Blue and Silver.
,, Harry Lee-tipper's	g.	a.	h.	*Daisy Bee*		9	0	Scarlet, White Cap.
,, Parker's	c.	a.	g.	*Peter Simple*		10	11	Scarlet, Black Sleeves and Cap.
,, A. Prince's	b.	a.	g.	*Kangaroo*		10	11	Red and White Stripes, Blue Cap.
,, do.	b.	a.	g.	*Looper*		9	0	Do. Do. Do.
,, Sam's	b.	a.	h.	*Marked Nag*		9	9	Dark Blue and Cherry Cap.
,, Tinchamberlain's	b.	a.	g.	*Cornhill*		10	11	Orange and Black Cap.

8.—THE SCRAMBLE.—Value Tls. 100.—For China and Japan PONIES.—Weight 10st. 7lbs.—Entrance Tls. 10 each.—Twice round a Course selected by the Committee.

Owner				Pony	st.	lb.	Colours
Mr. Edward's	[illegible]	[illegible]	p.	*Dun Deary*	10	7	Blue and Silver.
,, do.	[illegible]	[illegible]	p.	*[illegible]*	10	7	Do. Do.
,, Henry's	[illegible]	[illegible]	p.	*Our Mutual Friend*	10	7	Dark Blue and Black Cap.
,, Harry Lee-tipper's	w.	c.	p.	*[illegible]*	10	7	Scarlet, White Cap.
,, William's	[illegible]	c.	p.	*Delusion*	10	7	Lavender and Cherry.
,, do.	[illegible]	c.	p.	*Magician*	10	7	Do. Do.
,, Fungus'	[illegible]	c.	p.	*Feu de Joie*	10	7	Yellow, Black Sleeves and Cap.
,, Male-Ross'	[illegible]	c.	p.	*Boy Trotter*	10	7	Crimson, Saffron and Blue.
,, do.	w.	c.	p.	*Mendicant*	10	7	Do. Do.
,, do.	[illegible]	c.	p.	*Tinpan*	10	7	Do. Do.
,, Knowles'	[illegible]	c.	p.	*Colonel*	10	7	Orange and Black Cap.
,, Frank's	[illegible]	c.	p.	*Mr. Jorrocks*	10	7	Black and Magenta.
,, Alpha's	[illegible]	c.	p.	*[illegible]*	10	7	Pink.
,, Sigg's	[illegible]	c.	p.	*[illegible]*	10	7	Grey.
,, do.	[illegible]	c.	p.	*[illegible]*	10	7	Do.
,, Alexander's	[illegible]	c.	p.	*Ozone*	10	7	Magenta and Lemon Sleeves.
,, do.	[illegible]	c.	p.	*Tornado*	10	7	Do. Do.
,, Plume's	[illegible]	c.	p.	*[illegible]*	10	7	Blue Jacket, White Cap.
,, O'Leary's	[illegible]	c.	p.	*[illegible]*	10	7	Light Blue.
Lord Nonsense's	[illegible]	c.	p.	*[illegible]*	10	7	Violet and Straw.
Mr. Dawson's	[illegible]	c.	p.	*[illegible]*	10	7	Blue and White Hoops.
,, A. Prince's	[illegible]	c.	p.	*[illegible]*	10	7	Red and White Stripes, Blue Cap.
,, Trelly's	[illegible]	c.	p.	*[illegible]*	10	7	Lavender and Black.
,, Smallwood's	[illegible]	c.	p.	*The Rejected*	10	7	White, Scarlet Sash and Cap.
,, Southern's	[illegible]	c.	p.	*Meteor*	10	7	Scarlet, Yellow Cap.
,, Male-Ross'	bk.	c.	p.	*[illegible]*	10	7	Crimson, Saffron and Blue.

A. H. DE CARVALHO, PRINTER AND STATIONER.

上海跑马赛
彩票

Horse racing-themed raffle tickets issued in Shanghai

尺寸 /Size:
133mm × 120mm
年代 /Date:
1935

尺寸 /Size:
155mm × 110mm
年代 /Date:
1939

上海跑马厅
早期铜制门扣

Copper-made door holders
in the early days of
Shanghai Race Club

尺寸 /Size：
165mm × 265mm × 18mm
重量 /Weight：
1 730.6g，1 821g
年代 /Date：
近代 /Modern times

上海
万国竞走比赛
纪念奖杯
Commemorative trophy of Shanghai International Race Walking Competition

这是参加 1925 年上海万国竞走比赛的印度人 Otto Castonier 获得的纪念奖杯，他身披 34 号号码布，成绩为 2 小时 49 分 33 秒。奖杯纤小精致，双耳细长，口沿呈波浪状，杯身如同一支半开的花朵，杯身外壁刻有比赛名称、年份及获奖者姓名，设计简约古朴。

光绪三十年（1904），旅居上海的西方侨民发起的一项名为“万国竞走”的城市体育赛事，在每年冬季的一个星期日举行，民国元年（1911）暂停，1923 年恢复，1934 年终止，先后曾举办过 19 届。民国以前参赛者全部为外国侨民，按国籍分队，有法国、日本、美国、葡萄牙等队参赛，比赛设团体冠军及个人冠军。比赛路线以静安寺路（今南京西路）王家厍为起点，经静安寺路、极斯菲尔路（今万航渡路）、白利南路（今长宁路）、兆丰公园（今中山公园）、别罗根路（今哈密路）、虹桥路，由交通大学折回，沿姚主教路（今天平路）、贝当路（今衡山路）、辣斐德路（今复兴中路）、亚尔培路（今陕西南路）、福煦路（今陕西北路）经威海路入跑马厅，终点设在跑马厅的大看台前，全程 51 华里，规定 3 小时 20 分内走完。团体以英格兰队得冠军最多。万国竞走比赛是远东地区首屈一指的城市体育赛事，1928 年沪上英文报纸《北华捷报》誉之为“The Biggest Annual Athletic Contest of Any City in the Far East”，即“远东城市中最大的一项年度体育赛事”。1922 年，开始有中国人参加比赛的记载。1926 年，中国人组队参加万国竞走比赛，并取得了第二名的好成绩。1928 年，中华队第三次参赛就获得了团体和个人双料冠军。至 1933 年，中华队团体赛六连冠，个人赛六年五冠。其中个人冠军分别由周余愚、石金生、蔡正义所获。

□ The cup was awarded to Otto Castonier, an Indian who participated in the 1925 Shanghai World Walking race. He won the race by 2 hours, 49 minutes and 33 seconds, wearing a racing suit marked with "No. 34". The cup is small and delicate, with slender ears and the wavelike edge of its mouth. The body of the cup is like a half-open flower. Its outer wall is engraved with the name of the race, the year and name of the winner, designed in a simple and antique style.

□ In the 30th year of the reign of Emperor Guangxu (1904), an urban sports event called "World Walking Race" was launched by western residents living in Shanghai. It was held on a Sunday in winter every year. It was suspended in the first year of the Republic of China, resumed in 1923, and ended in 1934. A total of 19 sessions of the race were held successively. Before the Republic of China was founded, all contestants of this race were foreign residents. The teams were organized according to nationality. There were ever teams from France, Japan, the United States, Portugal and Jewish community. Group championship and individual championship were set up for the race. The racing route started from Wang Jiashe on Jing'an Temple Road (West Nanjing Road), passed through Jing'an Temple Road, Jessfield Road (Wanhangdu Road), Brenan Road (Changning Road), Jessfield Park (Zhongshan Park), Rubicon Road (Hami Road) and Hongqiao Road to Shanghai Jiao Tong University, then turned back along Route Prosper Paris (Tianping Road), Route Petain (Hengshan Road), Route Lafayette (Fuxing Middle Road), Route Albert (South Shaanxi Road), Avenue Foch (North Shaanxi Road), Weihai Road and ended at the front of the grandstand of Shanghai Race Club. The whole course was 25.5 kilometers long, and the contestants were required to finish the race within the time of 3 hours and 20 minutes. England Team won with the most times of championship. As the first urban sporting event in the Far East, Shanghai World Walking Race was honored as "The Biggest Annual Athletic Contest of Any City in the Far East" in 1928 by *North-China Herald*, an English newspaper in Shanghai. From 1922, there were the records of Chinese participating in the race. In 1926, Chinese Team participated in the race and came second to the championship. In 1928, Chinese Team won both team and individual championships when attending the race for the third time. By 1933, the Chinese team had won the team championship for the 6th year in a row and 5 individual championships in 6 years. The individual championships were respectively won by Zhou Yuyu, Shi Jinsheng and Cai Zhengyi.

尺寸 /Size:
210mm × 90mm × 210mm
重量 /Weight:
390.5g
年代 /Date:
1925

上海赛艇比赛冠军奖杯

Champion trophy of Shanghai Rowing Competition

□ 1878年5月9日下午，上海划船总会举行春季赛艇比赛，比赛项目包括八人单桨有舵手、双人双桨无舵手的比赛。在男子八人单桨有舵手的比赛中，红队以5分59秒获得胜利，这是本场比赛的奖杯。奖杯器型高挑端庄，由杯盖和杯身两部分组成，杯盖顶部立有一位手持赛艇划桨的外籍绅士像，点明赛艇会主题。杯身外壁及双耳皆錾刻各种花卉纹样，双耳内侧饰有乳钉纹浅浮雕，奖杯正中刻有表示比赛名称、年份及获奖队伍选手姓名。杯足由三支细长的赛艇划桨交错而成。奖杯设计构思巧妙，做工精湛。

□ 上海是中国近代赛艇运动的摇篮。1852年，一群外侨青年在黄浦江畔组织了一场设有赛艇和帆船两个项目的赛艇会，是我国第一场有正式记载的赛艇比赛。1859年，“上海划船总会”的前身“上海赛艇会”成立。1863年5月1日，在上海运动事业基金会（又称“万国体育会”）的贷款支持下，上海划船总会正式成立，会址在苏州河石桥西首。随后，形式多样的赛艇比赛和活动逐渐形成规模。每年春、秋各一次的常规赛事，成为在沪外侨的盛会。

□ In the afternoon of May 9, 1878, Shanghai Rowing Club held a spring rowing race, including such events as a coxed eight-man single-oar match and a coxless pair-man double-oars match. During the men's coxed eight single-oar racing, the red team won by 5 minutes and 59 seconds. The cup takes a high shape of elegance, composed of a lid and a body. On the top of the lid stands a foreign gentleman holding an oar of a racing boat, making clear the theme of the rowing race. The outer wall and the ears of the body are carved with various floral patterns. The inner side of the ears is decorated with a bas-relief of breast-nail pattern. The surface of the middle of the body is carved with the inscriptions indicating the race name, the year and the names of members from the winning team. Three long and thin sweep-oar-like parts are crossed with one another to make up the foot of the cup which is designed with ingenuity in an exquisite way.

□ Shanghai is the cradle of modern Chinese rowing. In 1852, a group of young foreigners organized a rowing race with two events, rowing and sailing, on the banks of the Huangpu River. It was the first officially recorded rowing race in our country. In 1859, "Shanghai Rowing Club", the predecessor of "Shanghai Regatta Club", was established. On May 1, 1863, with the support of the loan from Shanghai Sports Foundation (also know as the "Universal Sports Association"), the Shanghai Rowing Club was formally established, and the venue was at the west end of the Suzhou River Stone Bridge. Subsequently, various forms of rowing race and activities gradually formed a scale. The regular events, held once in Spring and Autumn each year, have become a grand event of overseas Chinese.

尺寸 /Size：
230mm × 125mm × 380mm
重量 /Weight：
800.8g
年代 /Date：
1878

上海划船总会八人比赛奖杯

Trophy of the men's eight regatta held by the Shanghai Rowing Club

□ 由于杭州、福州各个俱乐部的队员不能参加，上海划船总会（SRC）不得不取消了1879年的春季划船比赛。在此年的5月26日举行了一个小规模的比赛代替例行的春季划船比赛。在八人单桨有舵手的比赛中，红队以6分2秒获得了比赛的胜利，这便是本场比赛的奖杯。奖杯器型厚重，与马克杯相似，杯身为锡制，杯底由玻璃制成，杯面光滑无花纹，仅在外壁及足底刻有铭文，底部厂铭"James Dixon & Sons"，杯身刻有比赛名称、年份及获奖队伍选手姓名。红队的舵手是Hall，领桨手是Andrew，1号位桨手是Dumaresq。

□ Shanghai Rowing Club (SRC) had to cancel the spring rowing race in 1879 because the team members of various clubs in Hangzhou and Fuzhou could not be in attendance. On May 26 in that year, a small-size rowing race was held in place of the regular spring rowing race. In the coxed eight-man single-oar race, the red team won by 6 minutes and 2 seconds. The cup is heavy, similar to a mug. The body of the cup is made of tin, with the base being made of glass. Its surface is smooth and free of patterns. Only on its outer wall and base are engraved with inscriptions. The base is engraved with the manufacturer "James Dixon & Sons," and the body is engraved with the race name, the year and the names of members from the winning team. The cox of the red team is Hall, the leading rower is Andrew, and the rower on the No.1 position is Dumaresq.

尺寸 /Size:
130mm × 100mm × 125mm
重量 /Weight:
472.1g
年代 /Date:
1879

美国 Dyker Meadow 高尔夫俱乐部比赛奖杯
Trophy of Dyker Meadow Golf Club

□ The cup is simple in design, with its both ears and foot in background color. Its body is brownish red, with a club logo on its outer wall presented in the form of fire paint. The inscriptions read "DYKER MEADOW GOLF CLUB, MEDAL HANDICAP LABOR DAY 1907" and "J-E-WAY" (the name of the winner). On its base is shown its serial number "1142" and the place of its production "New York".

□ 这是美国Dyker Meadow高尔夫俱乐部比赛的奖杯，奖杯器型设计简约质朴，双耳和杯足维持原色，杯身呈棕红色，外壁带有俱乐部徽标，以火漆印的样式呈现，鏨刻铭文"DYKER MEADOW GOLF CLUB，MEDAL HANDICAP LABOR DAY 1907"和获奖者名字"J-E-WAY"，底部有编号1142和产地纽约。

尺寸 /Size:
200mm × 110mm × 174mm
重量 /Weight:
474g
年代 /Date:
1907

上海高尔夫俱乐部 A 等冠军奖杯

A-Champion trophy of Shanghai Golf Club

这是上海高尔夫俱乐部 A 等冠军奖杯，杯身刻有中国传统的龙纹和“上海高尔夫俱乐部 1929–30 赛季”“江湾十二月月度竞赛” “A 等”等字样。

1894 年，18 名外侨发起成立上海高尔夫俱乐部（上海杓球总会），球场设于今人民广场的跑马场。1911 年，上海万国体育会在江湾跑马场处筹建 18 洞高尔夫球场，上海高尔夫俱乐部聘请了驻场职业球手，并帮助管理江湾球场建设及后期工作。1912 年 12 月，上海高尔夫俱乐部正式宣布球场开放。1923 年，上海高尔夫俱乐部开始接受中国人成为会员。1925 年，第一届中国高尔夫公开赛在江湾高尔夫球场举行。1932 年，江湾球场部分受到战火破坏。后被日军占领，这座位于江湾的高尔夫球场便由此消失。

This is the A-Champion trophy of Shanghai Golf Club. The cup is engraved with a Chinese traditional pattern of dragon and some characters such as “Shanghai Golf Club 1929-30 Season”, “Jiangwan Monthly Competition in December”, “Grade A” and so on.

In 1894, 18 foreigners initiated the establishment of the Shanghai Golf Club (Shanghai Dipper Ball Club Field), which was Located in the racecourse of People’s Square. In 1911, the Shanghai World Sports Association built an 18-hole golf course at the Jiangwan Racecourse. The Shanghai Golf Club hired resident professional golfers to help manage the construction and Later worked of the Jiangwan Course. In December 1912, the Shanghai Golf Club officially announced the opening of the course. In 1923, the Shanghai Golf Club began to accept Chinese as members. In 1925, the first China Golf Open was held at Jiangwan Golf course. In 1932, Jiangwan Golf course was partially damaged by war. After being occupied by the Japanese army, this golf course in Jiangwan Disappeared.

尺寸 /Size：
130mm × 95mm × 140mm
重量 /Weight：
715g
年代 /Date：
1929

上海瑞士国洋枪打靶会奖杯

Trophies of Swiss Rifle Club

□ 这组奖杯为 20 世纪二三十年代上海瑞士国洋枪打靶会射击比赛的银质奖杯。

□ 八件奖杯器型皆为典型的欧式奖杯式样，带有双耳，素面无纹，部分外壁錾刻铭文“Swiss Rifle Club”。奖杯原盒包装印有公司名 ZEE SUNG&CO，以及公司地址等信息。

□ 早期上海的外国侨民的身份多为半兵半商，故上海自 1843 年开埠以来，早期经上海流入中国的现代体育运动项目也多有军营背景，如最早开展的马术与射击。在外国侨民的影响下，清末民初，上海逐步成立了上海射击俱乐部及各国射击俱乐部等多个军民混合组织，并定期举办射击比赛。

□ 1911 年，为满足在沪瑞士侨民洋枪打靶的需要，上海瑞士国洋枪打靶会 (Swiss Rifle Club) 成立，每年举办年度射击比赛。1921 年，上海瑞士国洋枪打靶会发展为瑞士总会 (Swiss Club)，总部设于上海吕西纳路 (今利西路) 21 号，对外仍使用打靶会的名号。1928 年，打靶会正式改名为瑞士总会，总会成为瑞士在沪侨民的主要聚会场所，同时发挥着社交联络、凝聚社区与体育娱乐活动的功能。

□ This collection of trophies being made of silver are for shooting competitions organized by Shanghai Swiss Rifle Club in the 1920s and 1930s.

□ The eight trophies are all of the typical European styles with double ears and plain faces free of patterns. The external sides of some trophies are engraved with the inscription “Swiss Rifle Club.” The LOGO of the paper boxes is printed with the company name ZEE SUNG & CO and the company address.

□ Since the opening of the port in the 1840s,many foreign immigrants in Shanghai were both military officials and merchants. Thus, the modern sports that were introduced into China via Shanghai in the early days were also of military characteristics, for example, the earliest introduced equestrian and shooting. Influenced by the foreign immigrants, between the end of the Qing Dynasty and the beginning of the Republic of China, Shanghai gradually established a number of military-civilian organizations such as Shanghai Rifle Club and other countrics' Rifle Clubs, which regularly held shooting competitions.

□ In 1911, in order to meet the needs of the Swiss expatriates in Shanghai to shoot with foreign guns, Swiss Rifle Club was established to hold an annual shooting competition every year. In 1921, Swiss Rifle Club developed into Swiss club, its headquarters at No.21 Lucina Road (Lixi Road), Shanghai, and the name of the Rifle Club is still used externally. In 1928, Swiss Rifle Club officially changed its name to Swiss Club, which became the main meeting place for Swiss expatriates in Shanghai, and at the same time played the functions of social contact, community cohesion and sports & entertainment activities.

一组 8 件（7 件带原盒）
A collection of eight trophies
(seven of which are placed in the original boxes)
尺寸，重量 /Size，Weight：
60mm × 85mm × 60mm，233.2g
45mm × 82mm × 107mm，116.6g
60mm × 105mm × 125mm，134.4g
60mm × 90mm × 70mm，177g
80mm × 138mm × 102mm，208.2g
51mm × 95mm × 106mm，91.7g
60mm × 117mm × 130mm，194.6g
54mm × 85mm × 120mm，114.4g
年代 /Date：
1920s–1930s

美国业余体育联合会游泳比赛金牌

Gold medal of the swimming competition held by Amateur Athletic Union of the United States

□ 奖牌正面为手持橄榄枝环的女神，并刻有“美国业余体育联合会”的英文字样和以罗马数字显示的联合会成立年份“1888”。背面为各种体育器械和花朵组成的圆环图案，中间刻有“50码游泳，1908”的数字和英文字样，并刻有夺金运动员的名字“Marquard Schwarz”（马奎德·施瓦兹）。

□ 马奎德·施瓦兹（1887—1968）美国著名短道游泳选手，毕业于耶鲁大学，效力于密苏里体育俱乐部。参加过1904年圣路易斯奥运会和1906年雅典奥运会（非正式）。在1904年奥运会上获得4×50米游泳接力比赛铜牌。

□ The medal has a goddess holding an olive branch and is engraved with the words “American Amateur Swimming Tournament” on the front. The back is a ring composed of various kinds of sports equipment and flowers, with the number and English words “50-yard swimming 1908” engraved in the middle and the name of the gold medalist “Marquard Schwarz”.

□ Marquard Schwarz (1887-1968), famous American short course swimmer, graduated from Yale University and worked for the Missouri Athletic Club. He participated in the St. Louis 1904 Summer Olympics and the 1906 Intercalated Games held in Athens. He won the bronze medal of 4×50m relay in the St. Louis 1904 Summer Olympics.

尺寸 /Size：

Φ40mm × 3mm

重量 /Weight：

30.8g

年代 /Date：

1908

上海游泳同乐会比赛奖杯

Competition trophy of S.A.S.A.

□ 这是1933年上海游泳同乐会举办比赛女子50码自由泳冠军J.Ball的奖杯。奖杯外壁刻有铭文：S.A.S.A. SHANGHAI Ladies' 50yd. Free Style Championship 1933 J.BALL，足部有厂铭"昌""SEESUNGSSILVER"，为上海广帮银楼"时新"号。奖杯侈口、束颈，双耳呈几何造型，素面无纹。

□ 上海游泳同乐会（简称S.A.S.A.）成立于1914年8月6日，旨在促进上海游泳技艺。该会采用英格兰业余游泳俱乐部规则，会员必须是上海某个已经得到认可的游泳俱乐部会员。1930年代上海游泳同乐会办公室一度设于公共租界工部局税务署。该会主要领导由法国球场俱乐部、上海游泳俱乐部、上海西侨青年会、上海跑马俱乐部等俱乐部领导构成。上海游泳同乐会成立后，协调组织上海市内重大游泳比赛。1931年、1934年、1935年，上海与香港、天津的埠际游泳比赛，均为上海游泳同乐会主办。

□ This is the trophy won by J.Ball, who was the champion of S.A.S.A. Women's 50yd Freestyle Swimming Competition in 1933. The external side is engraved with the inscription S.A.S.A. SHANGHAI Ladies' 50yd. Free Style Championship 1933 J.BALL; the base is engraved with the manufacturer inscription of the Chinese character " 昌 " (prosperous) and the inscription "SEESUNGSSILVER", which is the most popular inscription of Shanghai Guangbang Silverware Shop. The trophy has a wide mouth, a thin neck, two ears of geometrical shapes and plain faces free of patterns.

□ Shanghai Amateur Swimming Association, abbreviated to S.A.S.A., was founded on August 6, 1914, which aimed to promote swimming skills in Shanghai. It adopted the rules of England Amateur Swimming Club. The members must be registered as members in accredited swimming clubs in Shanghai. In the 1930s, the office of S.A.S.A. was set in the Tax Department of Shanghai Municipal Council in Shanghai International Settlement. S.A.S.A. was mainly led by managers of clubs including French Field Club, Shanghai Swimming Club, Shanghai Foreign YMCA and Shanghai Racecourse Club. After its establishment, it coordinated and organized the major swimming competitions in Shanghai. In 1931, 1934 and 1935, the inter-port swimming competitions among Shanghai, Hong Kong and Tianjin were all hosted by S.A.S.A.

尺寸 /Size:
150mm × 70mm × 120mm
重量 /Weight:
137g
年代 /Date:
1933

美国艾奥瓦州麋鹿俱乐部年度冠军奖杯

Champion Trophy of IOWA STATE MOOSE ASS'N ROTATION, the United States

□ 这是美国艾奥瓦州麋鹿俱乐部年度冠军奖杯，分为上下两部分，上半部分为运动员雕塑，精制镀金，耸立在浮雕着橄榄枝的基座上，双手高举，一只手握着橄榄枝花环。立体的“小金人”雕刻得既圆润又处处棱角分明，鞋带、头发等处处都是精雕细琢，形象逼真。奖杯的下部原是光滑如镜的黄铜，已氧化成古朴的古铜色，上刻有“IOWA STATE MOOSE ASS'N ROTATION CHAMPION 1948”字样。奖杯底部有制作公司道奇的徽标。

□ This is the annual champion trophy of Iowa State Moose Ass'n Rotation in the United States, which is divided into the upper and lower parts. The upper part is the sculpture of athletes, refined and gold plated, standing on the base of the embossed olive branch, with both hands highly raised and one hand holding the olive wrench. The three-dimensional "golden man" is delicately carved with clear-cut shoelaces and hair, exquisite and vivid. It is an exquisite artwork of sports and cultural relics. The lower part of the trophy was originally made of brass as smooth as a mirror, which has been oxidized to pale bronze, engraved with the English words "IOWA STATE MOOSE ASS'N ROTATION CHAMPION 1948". The bottom of the trophy has a logo of its producer Dodge.

尺寸 /Size:
Φ200mm × 550mm
重量 /Weight:
1 810.1g
年代 /Date:
1948

英国乒乓球拍、球网、乒乓球

British table tennis bats, nets, table tennis balls

□ 这是英国维多利亚时代的一组乒乓球套装，包含原装乒乓球单打球拍 1 对（2 个）、球网和木质球网支架及金属固定装置，以及乒乓球 3 只。乒乓球拍手柄长而细，用来击球的板面由羊皮制成，中间空心。

□ 乒乓球运动于 19 世纪末起源于英国。最初只是一种活动性游戏，球是用轻而富有弹性的材料（如软木、橡胶）制成，拍子是雪茄烟盒盖之类的木质板，像打网球那样在桌上打，故欧洲人称之为“桌上网球”。1900 年左右，由于轻工业的发展，球才改用赛璐珞制成的空心球。此后，乒乓球运动才逐步发展起来。20 世纪初，上海一家文具店的老板从日本买回十套乒乓球用于推广，由此乒乓球运动从上海向全国普及。

□ This is a set of table tennis set from the Victorian era in England. In clouding one pair 2 of original table tennis singles rackets, het and wooden net bracket and metal fixing device, and 3 table tennis balls. The handle of a table tennis racket is long and thin, and the board used to hit the ball is made of sheepskin with a hollow center.

□ Table tennis originated in England at the end of the 19th century. It was originally just an active game. The ball was made of light and elastic materials (such as cork and rubber), and the racket was a wooden board such as a cigar box. It was played on the table like tennis, so it was called “table tennis” by Europeans. Around 1900, due to the development of light industry, the ball was changed to a hollow ball made of celluloid. Since then, table tennis has gradually developed. At the beginning of the 20th century, the owner of a stationery store in Shanghai bought ten sets of table tennis balls from Japan for promotion, and the sport of table tennis spread from Shanghai to the whole country.

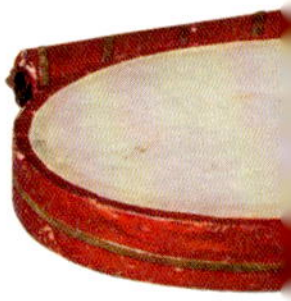

尺寸 /Size：
乒乓球拍 /Table tennis bats：
370mm × 122mm × 20mm
球网 /Nets：
290mm × 150mm × 70mm
乒乓球 /Table tennis balls：
Φ38mm
年代 /Date：
维多利亚时代 /Victorian Era

冰鞋

A pair of skates

□ This is a pair of mid-20th century ice skates with a high-waisted hard sole, made of high quality cowhide leather and lined with fleece inside. The word "Clipper" and "Olympic Quality" are engraved at the joint of the blade and the skates. The blade is made of steel and is tall but short, basically the same length as the skates, with a certain curvature. The blade and the holder are integrated and the blade is thick and rounded. These skates are generally used for ice hockey.

□ 这是一双20世纪中叶的冰鞋，鞋身高腰硬底，采用优质牛皮制成，内部衬有绒毛。刀身和鞋的连接处刻有“Clipper”和“Olympic Quality”字样。冰刀为钢制，刀身高且短，基本和鞋的长度一致，有一定弧度。刀刃和刀托为一体，刀刃较厚，呈圆弧状。此类冰鞋一般用于冰球运动。

尺寸 /Size：
39码
年代 /Date：
1950s–1960s

门球

A set of Croquet Tools

□ This is an early set of croquet tools, including 6 iron ring gates, 2 finishing posts, 2 mallets and 2 balls.

□ Croquet is an outdoor ball game in which players using mallets drive wooden balls through a series of wickets set out on a lawn. Originated from France, croquet was transmitted into Britain in the 13th century, and then into Italy in the 17th century before coming to the US. By 1930s when introduced into China, it was only played in Yenching University as a sports game. Croquet gained great popularity in Japan in 1948 and began to be promoted as an activity for the elderly nationwide in 1970.

□ 这是早期的一套门球器械，含有铁环门 6 个、终点柱 2 个、木槌 2 把和球 2 枚。

□ 门球是在平地或草坪上，用木槌击打球穿过铁门的一种室外球类游戏，又称槌球。门球起源于法国，13 世纪传入英国，17 世纪传入意大利，此后传到美国。20 世纪 30 年代传入中国，当时只在燕京大学作为游戏课内容。1948 年门球在日本兴起 ，1970 年开始作为老年人的活动项目在中国推广开来。

尺寸 /Size:
铁环门 /Iron ring gates:
246mm × 46mm × 245mm
终点柱 /Finishing posts:
43mm × 225mm
木槌 /Mallets:
708mm × 50mm × 120mm
球 /Balls:
Φ60mm
年代 /Date:
近代 /Modern times

民国时期
第五届全运会奖杯
Trophy of the 5th National Games in the period of the Republic of China

□ 民国时期第五届全运会奖杯器型厚重古朴，似香炉状。杯盖为网状结构，杯身口沿以窃曲纹及连枝纹装饰，下方印有“我武维扬”字样，以表率运动员在全运会上的卓越成就，双耳被设计成鸟雀的形象，别有意趣。奖杯由福建省政府捐赠给全运会组委会，后颁发给在本届全运会上获得80米低栏冠军的上海运动员钱行素。

□ The trophy of the 5th National Games in the period of the Republic of China is thick and classically elegant in the shape similar to a censer. The lid is like a net. The mouth is decorated with curred and continuous patterns. The Chinese characters " 我武维扬 " (Powerful) are printed at the bottom to show the excellent achievements of athletes in the Games. The ears were designed like birds, which are of unique significance. It was donated by the Fujian Provincial Government, then awarded to Qian Xingsu, a Shanghai athlete who won the 80m low hurdles champion at this National Games.

尺寸 /Size:

300mm × 180mm × 280mm

重量 /Weight:

1 835.9g

捐赠者 /Donated by:

陈世和 / Chen Shihe

年代 /Date:

1933

钱行素（1915—1968），上海嘉定人。1930 年考入上海东亚体育师范学校附属高中师范学校，毕业后直升体专。1931 年 9 月，在上海市第二届运动会上，钱行素获女子 200 米和跳远冠军，并创全国新纪录。翌年 10 月，上海举行万国运动会，钱行素以中华队队员身份参加 4×100 米接力赛跑，持第一棒，起步极快，中华女队以 58 秒成绩获得冠军。1933 年 9 月，在上海市第三届运动会上，创女子 100 米、200 米赛跑的全国纪录。10 月，代表上海参加在南京举行的第五届全国运动会，获女子 100 米 (13 秒 5)、200 米 (27 秒 6)、80 米低栏 (14 秒 5)、4×100 米接力 (54 秒 6) 的冠军和跳远亚军，并创 4 项全国新纪录。上海《时事新报》全运会特刊曾作专题报道，国民政府考试院特颁锦旗以表彰。1934 年，应华侨领袖陈嘉庚、胡文虎等人的邀请，组织“东亚南游团”，一行 10 人，钱行素为团长，赴新加坡、槟榔屿、吉隆坡等地巡回表演，受到当地华侨的欢迎。1935 年在上海举行的第六届全运会上，钱行素又获 80 米低栏第一名。1936 年毕业后，历任上海务本、明德、启秀、智仁勇等女中及大同大学、暨南大学及母校体专体育教师，兼任上海市高校学生田径队指导。1950 年，调任复旦大学体育讲师。

C… ip of women's 100m race (13'5''),
b… 0m race (27'6''), women's 80m low
I… '') and women's 4X100m relay (54'6''),
t… e runner-up of women's long jump,
S… new national records. The special
As… ational Games of The China Times
Af… l reports for the achievements and
di… ion Institute of Nanjing National
Co… also issued her a silk banner in
at … her wonderful performance. In
Sh… by leaders of Chinese overseas
ch… ding Chen Jiageng and Hu Wenhu,
rac… rganized and led the "East Asian
cre… m" consisting of ten team members
In O… such as Singapore, Penang Island
held… pur. They were well received by
Qian… se overseas nationals. At the 6th
wom… s held in Shanghai in 1935, Qian
as a… first place in women's 80m low
team… ter her graduation in 1936, she
baton… rked as a physical education
enabl… e secondary schools such as
team… , Mingde, Qixiu and Zhirenyong,
with a… g University, Jinan University and
In Sep… he sports college. At the same
Sports… ovided guidance for Shanghai
she br… athletics teams. In 1950, she
women… o Fudan University as a lecturer
200m r… tion.
particip…
Games…
of Shan…

民国时期
第六届全运会奖杯

Trophy of the 6th National Games in the period of the Republic of China

The Trophy of the 6th National Games in the period of the Republic of China is shaped like a vividly running athlete, whose eyes are like the torch with a determined look. It was donated by Cai Yuanpei, the President of Academia Sinica, then awarded to Qian Xingsu, a Shanghai athlete who won the 80m low hurdles champion at this National Games.

民国时期第六届全运会奖杯杯身为一位奔跑状的运动员形象，运动员目光如炬，神情坚毅，栩栩如生。杯座上刻有铭文“光臻华国”。奖杯由时任中央研究院院长蔡元培赠予全运会组委会，后颁发给在本届运动会上获得 80 米低栏冠军的上海运动员钱行素。

尺寸 /Size：
Φ90mm × 230mm
重量 /Weight：
673.4g
捐赠者 /Donated by：
陈世和 / Chen Shihe
年代 /Date：
1935

上海圣约翰大学“见义勇为”奖杯

Shanghai St. John's University “Donating Thick Clothes against Cold Campaign” Trophy

□ 1939年，中华全国体育协进会总干事沈嗣良为褒奖圣约翰大学在抗日战争时期“劝募寒衣运动”颁赠的奖杯。奖杯器型简洁古朴，为典型的欧式纪念杯形状，素面无纹，表面錾刻铭文“廿八年约大劝募寒衣运动”“见义勇为”及“沈嗣良赠”字样。

□ 圣约翰大学是最早引进西方近代体育的学校，在体育水平与体育设施方面都是当时一流的。光绪十六年（1890）举办以田径为主的学校运动会，是中国体育史上最早出现的近代体育运动会。圣约翰大学1883—1909年先后修建了网球场、足球场、田径场等。1909年由校友会捐银一万两，购置土地建造有440码跑道和6个分道的220码直道的田径场，是大学中建造最早的正规田径场之一。1919年落成的圣约翰大学顾斐德（F.CIEMENL COOPER）纪念体育室是中国第一个现代化大学体育馆，内有健身房、球场、室内游泳池，为当时罕有。体育室基地面积421平方米，建筑面积881平方米。第一层有来宾接待室一间，以及浴室、更衣室、机房。第二层是室内运动场，长75英尺，宽45英尺。体育设备，始臻完善。

□ In 1939, Wm.Z.L.Sung, Director General of All-China Federation of Sports Associations, awarded the “Donating Thick Clothes against Cold Campaign” of St. John University during the War of Resistance against Japanese Aggression. The trophy is of simply ancient style, which is shaped like a typical European memorial cup with no patterns on the plain surface. The inscriptions on the surface are “Year 28 of the Republic of China, Donating Thick Clothes against Cold Campaign of St. John University”, “Act bravely for a just cause” and “Donated by Wm.Z.L.Sung”.

□ St. John's University was the first school to introduce modern western sports. It was the top in terms of sports competitiveness and sports facilities. In the 16th year of Emperor Guangxu's reign (1890), the school sports meeting held mainly for Athletics by St. John's University was the earliest modern sports event in Chinese sports history. From 1883 to 1909, St. John's University successively built tennis courts and football fields, as well as grounds for Athletics. In 1909, the Alumni Association donated 10,000 taels of silver to purchase land for a Athletics ground with 440-yard runways and 220-yard straight roads in 6 separate lanes, which was one of the earliest formal grounds built among universities. The F.CIEMENL COOPER Memorial Stadium, which was completed in 1919, is the first modern university gymnasium in China, with the gymnasium, stadium and indoor swimming pool inside, which was rare at that time. The base of the stadium covers an area of 421m^2 and a building area of 881m^2. On the first floor, there is a guest reception room, bathroom, locker and machine room. On the second floor, there is an indoor playground that is 75ft long and 45ft wide. There are diverse sports equipment, which are well-preserved.

尺寸 /Size：
80mm × 45mm × 85mm
重量 /Weight：
70.9g
年代 /Date：
1939

美国基督教青年会篮球比赛奖杯

Trophy of Young Men's Christian Association (YMCA) Basketball Competition

□ 这个是美国基督教青年会 1937—1938 年篮球比赛的镀金奖杯。奖杯由上下两部分组成，上部分是一个耸立跃起并单手扣篮的运动员形象，运动员身形矫健、姿势优美、动作协调，其上的头发、衣服、鞋子都经过精雕细琢，形象逼真。运动员脚下是奖杯的基座，占据了整体几乎三分之二的高度，这让位于上面的运动员形象更加雄壮高大。基座上方有橄榄枝浮雕，下方有“基督教青年会 1937—1938”等字样。

□ 中国篮球运动早期经美国基督教青年会传入。张伯苓、王正廷、马约翰、董守义等中国早期体育领军人物都是由基督教青年会选派赴美留学，从而开启并加速了我国体育事业的发展。

□ This is the gold-plated trophy for the American 1937-1938 YMCA basketball game. The trophy consists of upper and lower parts. The upper part is an image of an athlete jumping up and throwing basket with one hand. He is robust, lithe and elegant. It is delicate, with hair, clothes and shoes. At the foot of the sports element is the pedestal of the trophy, occupying almost two-thirds of the height of the whole, which makes the athletes on it more majestic and tall. There is an olive branch relief above the pedestal and the words "YMCA 1937-1938" below.

□ In the early days, Chinese basketball was introduced by the American YMCA. Early Chinese sports leaders such as Chang Po-ling, C.T.Wang, John Ma, and Dong Shouyi were all selected by the YMCA to study in the United States, thus opening and accelerating our country's sports careers.

尺寸 /Size：
Φ180mm × 550mm
重量 /Weight：
1 470.9g
年代 /Date：
1937—1938

西侨青年会
篮球联赛冠军个人奖杯

Individual Champion Trophy of Foreign Young Men's Christian Association (Foreign YMCA) Basketball League

□ 此为1940—1941年西侨青年会举办第十三届篮球联赛颁发给获奖球员的奖杯。奖杯侈口、方肩，颈部较宽，两侧有耳，圈足，呈棕红色。表面镶刻有上海西侨青年会的会徽铭牌，下方写有“1940—1941年西侨青年会举办第十三届篮球联赛冠军”的英文字样。

□ 鸦片战争后，上海外侨日益增加。为给侨居上海的外国青年提供一个体育和生活娱乐活动场所，基督教青年会总干事、美国人费奇1925年起向社会各界募集款项，筹建西侨青年会会所，得到美国石油大王洛克菲勒、美国前驻华公使克兰、大来轮船公司老板大来以及众多旅沪美侨的热情回应。1926年西侨青年会大楼奠基。1928年6月29日体育馆落成并举办开幕典礼。1932年扩建成9层，约有250个房间，均附设私人浴室，会员可享受食宿优惠待遇。一到三层有打球房、游泳池、健身房等体育设施。大楼内篮球场是当时上海滩最好的室内篮球场。西侨青年会在体育馆建成后，每年召开篮球、排球的西青邀请赛或公开赛。由西侨组队参赛，华人队也可参加。预期至次年2月2日结束，比赛分甲乙两组，甲组9队，乙组8队，每周比赛8次，星期二、四各2次，星期六则4次，参观券价分4角、6角两种，收入款项，悉数作此次比赛费用。由于篮球房的设施比较先进，20世纪30年代成了上海篮球比赛中心场地。1938年开始，上海西侨青年会篮球比赛采用美国篮球比赛规则。

尺寸 /Size：
85mm × 57mm × 100mm
重量 /Weight：
104g
年代 /Date：
1940–1941

□ It was the trophy awarded for winners of the 13th Basketball League held by Foreign YMCA from 1940 to 1941. The cup has a wide mouth, square shoulder, wide neck, ears on both sides and ring feet and is brown-red. On the surface, there is a Foreign YMCA emblem label, and the English words of "Champion of the 13th Basketball League held by Foreign YMCA from 1940 to 1941" are engraved below.

□ After the Opium War, the number of overseas immigrants in Shanghai were ever-increasing. In order to provide a place for foreign youth living in Shanghai to play sports and enjoy life for fun, an American named Fitch, Director General of Foreign YMCA raised funds from all walks of life to build the office for the association since 1925. He received an enthusiastic response from the American petroleum giant Rockefeller, former American Ambassador to China Kilan, boss of Dalai Ship Company Dalai and many Americans living in Shanghai. In 1926, the Foreign YMCA building was founded. On June 29, 1928, the stadium was completed with an opening ceremony. In 1932, it was expanded into 9 floors, with about 250 rooms, all of which are attached with private bathrooms. The members can enjoy preferential treatment in catering and accommodation. There are sports facilities including courts, swimming pools and gyms from the first to the third floor. The basketball court inside the building was the best indoor basketball court in Shanghai at that time. After the establishment of the stadium, Foreign YMCA held invitation games or open games for basketball and volleyball every year. Foreigners participated in the games in the form of teams and Chinese were also allowed for engagement. The games were projected to end by February 2 of the next year. All the teams were divided into Group A and Group B. There were nine teams in Group A and eight in Group B, with eight games per week, two on Tuesdays and Thursdays, six on Saturdays. The prices of the tickets were 40 cents and 60 cents. All the revenues were used for the games. Due to the advanced facilities in the basketball court, it was used as the core venue for basketball games in Shanghai in the 1930s. Since 1938, basketball games held by Shanghai Foreign YMCA adopted the rules of basketball games of the United States.

上海—松江竞走比赛纪念章

Commemorative Badge for Shanghai-Songjiang Race Walking Competition

□ 此为周余愚1930年在沪参加上海—松江竞走比赛所获纪念章。

□ 周余愚（1908—1994），浙江宁波人，我国著名竞走运动员。1927年，周余愚在上海万国竞走比赛中夺得青年组个人冠军，此后四年与队友一直垄断该比赛的团体和个人双料冠军。在比赛期间，周余愚与朋友组织成立了中华竞走会，在上海屡创佳绩，引起了当时中国体育最高主管机构——中华全国体育协进会的关注。1934年，协进会通知中国竞走会委托其负责选拔队员参加奥运会竞走比赛。周余愚因成绩突出，入选奥运中国代表团。

□ 1936年，周余愚代表中国参加第十一届柏林夏季奥运会竞走比赛，获姿势优美奖。

□ This is the commemorative badge of Zhou Yuyu's engagement in Shanghai-Songjiang Race Walking 1930.

□ Zhou Yuyu (1908-1994), born in Ningbo, Zhejiang province, is a famous Chinese race walking athlete. In 1927, Zhou Yuyu won the individual championship of the youth group in the Shanghai World Race Walking competition, and he and his teammates have been monopolizing the team and individual double championship in the competition for the next four years. During the competition, Zhou Yuyu and his friends established the Chinese Race Walking Federation, which achieved great results in Shanghai. which attracted the attention of the China National Amateur Athletic Federation, the highest governing organization. In 1934, the Federation notified the China Race Walking Federation to entrust the selection of team members to participate in the Olympic games walking competition. Zhou Yuyu was selected for the Olympic delegation due to his outstanding achievements.

□ In 1936, Zhou Yuyu represented China at the 11th Summer Olympics in Berlin and won the award for graceful posture in the race walking competition.

尺寸 /Size:
25mm × 50mm × 1mm
重量 /Weight:
8.6g
捐赠者 /Donated by:
周明辉 /Zhou Minghui
年代 /Date:
1930

中华竞走会
男女公开赛纪念章

Commemorative Badge of the Open Tournament of Chinese Race Walking Association

□ 纪念章由上海著名商人程贻泽赠给中华竞走会男女公开赛举办方。纪念章正面为一个竞走造型的运动员形象，背面刻有比赛名称、时间、纪念章捐赠人和制作公司的信息。

□ 在租界外侨万国竞走运动比赛影响下，上海华人参加竞走比赛热情高涨。1926年，华人开始参加万国竞走比赛。中国现代第一个竞走体育组织中华竞走会于1930年春在上海成立，其前身为1926年张造寸等创办的“中华竞走队”。该会宗旨是倡导、推动竞走运动，为国人争气。程贻泽任名誉会长，主要成员有张造寸、陆雨田、王明职、周余愚等人。址设于威海卫路（今威海路）一家老虎灶内。次年，迁至西藏路（今西藏中路）慕尔堂。该会成立后，创设13英里竞走比赛，比赛路线以王家库（今南京西路石门一路转角处）为起点，向西经静安寺路（今南京西路）、极司菲尔路（今万航渡路）、白利南路（今长宁路）到达终点天文台路（今合肥路）中华运动场。每年定期举行，推动了竞走运动的发展，数支竞走队在上海相继成立，其中沪西队、晨光队、工部局俱乐部队、慕尔队和健恩队等，都具有较高水平。1934年，举办上海市20公里和50公里远距离竞走大赛；1936年，该会会员周余愚、蔡正义等入选中国代表队，参加第十一届柏林夏季奥运会。1942年太平洋战争爆发后，该会将所余经费委托上海《申报》社用以支援抗战，宣布停止活动，该会解散。

The badge was presented to the organizers of the Chinese Open Men's and Women's Race Walking Championships by renowned Shanghai businessman Cheng Yize. On the front of the badge is an image of an athlete in the shape of a race walker, and on the back is engraved the name of the race, the time, the donor of the badge and the company that made it.

Influenced by the World Race Walking competition launched by foreign nationals in the foreign settlement, Shanghai citizens became passionate about race walking. In 1926, Chinese people also began to participate in the World Race Walking. The first modern sports association for race walking was founded in Shanghai in the spring of 1930, formerly known as the "China Race Walking Team" established by Zhang Zaocun and others in 1926. It aimed to promote race walking and fight for the honor of China. Cheng Yize was the Honorary President and the main members included Zhang Zaocun, Lu Yutian, Wang Mingzhi, Zhou Yuyu, etc. It was set in a Laohuzao (boiled water store) on Weihai Port Road (now Weihai Road). One year later, it was moved to Moore Memorial Church on Xizang Road (now Middle Xizang Road). After its establishment, it launched a 13-mile race walking competition. The route started from Wangjiashe (a corner of Shimen First Road and West Nanjing Road) and ended at China Stadium on Tianwentai Road (now Hefei Road), passing by Jing'an Temple Road (now West Nanjing Road), Jisifeier Road (now Wanhangdu Road) and South Baili Road (now Changning Road) in the west direction. It was held regularly every year to promote the development of race walking. Several teams had been established in Shanghai successively, including the Shanghai West Team, Chenguang Team, Club Team of Shanghai Municipal Council, Moore Team and Jian'en Team, all of which were at a high level. In 1934, Shanghai 20km and 50km long-distance race walking competitions were held; in 1936, members including Zhou Yuyu and Cai Zhengyi were selected into the Chinese team to participate in the Berlin 1936 Olympic Games. After the outbreak of the Pacific War in 1942, the Association entrusted the remaining funds to Shanghai Shun Pao (Shanghai News) to support the War of Resistance against the Japanese Aggression, declaring the cessation of its activities and dissolution of the Association.

尺寸 /Size:
35mm × 35mm × 2mm
重量 /Weight:
13.8g
捐赠者 /Donated by:
程贻泽 /Cheng Yize
年代 /Date:
1934

民国时期
第六届全运会
纪念章

Commemorative medal of the 6th National Games in the period of the Republic of China

□ 纪念章正面是挥舞旗帜的运动员形象，上方写有“第六届全国运动大会”字样，背面是肩生双翼的男子飞跃于第六届全运会举办地上海市体育场（现上海市江湾体育场）的景象。

□ 1935 年 10 月 10—20 日，第六届全国运动会在上海市体育场举行。这是首次按照国民政府教育部颁布的《全国运动大会举行办开幕式表演法》举办的全国运动会。共有 38 支队伍、2285 名运动员参加了此次运动会。为了更好地与世界接轨，本次比赛将田径赛分为田赛和径赛。此外还设有游泳、篮球、排球、足球、网球、棒球等项目。其中，国术在全国运动会中首次设立锦标。大会还设举重、跳水、竞走、马球、小足球、蒙古式摔跤、自行车等表演项目。上海队分别获得男子组、女子组总分第一。

□ On the front side of the badge is the image of a sportsman flying the flag, with the words “the 6th National Games” on the top. At the back is a man with twin wings jumping in Jiangwan Stadium, the venue for the 6th National Games in the period of the Republic of China.

□ From October 10 to 20, 1935, the 6th National Games was held in the Shanghai Municipal Stadium. This is the first national sports game organized in accordance with *the Code Conduct for the Opening Ceremony of the National Games* issued by the Ministry of Education of the national government of the Republic of China. A total of 38 teams and 2,285 athletes participated in the National Games. In order to better communicate with the world, the athletics competitions were divided into field competitions and track competitions respectively. Besides, there were also sports including swimming, basketball, volleyball, soccer, tennis, baseball, etc. Among the sports, it was the first time to hold championship for martial arts in National Games. The Games also set up some demonstration sports such as weight lifting, diving, race walking, polo, soccer, Mongolian wrestling and cycling. The Shanghai team topped the scores for both the men’s team and the women’s team.

尺寸 /Size：
Φ70mm × 3mm
重量 /Weight：
93.9 克
捐赠者 /Donated by：
陈世和 /Chen Shihe
年代 /Date：
1935

民国时期
第七届全运会
第一名奖章

First place medal at the 7th National Games in the period of the Republic of China

□ 奖牌正面上半部分刻有“第七届全国运动大会第一名”字样，下半部分为由橄榄枝团簇的“全运会”铭文。背面是一排弯弓射箭、蓄势待发的运动员形象。

□ 1948年5月5—16日，民国时期第七届全国运动会在上海市江湾体育场举办。参加这届运动会的除32个省市外，还有陆军、海军、空军、联勤、警察和香港以及美国檀香山、暹罗、菲律宾、马来亚、越南西贡、仰光等国家和地区的华侨等共58个代表队2 670名成员。台湾省首次参赛。比赛项目设男子田径、游泳、举重、拳击、摔角（摔跤）、篮球、排球、足球、乒乓球、网球、垒球；女子田径、游泳、摔角、篮球、排球、乒乓球、网球、垒球。

□ The upper part of the medal is engraved with the words“First place of the 7th National Games”, and the lower part is engraved with Chinese characters “National Games” clustered by olive branches. On the back is the image of a row of athletes with bows and arrows ready to go.

□ From May 5 to 16, 1948, the 7th National Games in the period of the Republic of China was held in Jiangwan Stadium, Shanghai. In addition to the 32 provinces and cities, the participants also included 58 teams and 2,670 members from the army, navy, air force, joint service, police and Hong Kong, as well as overseas Chinese from Honolulu, Siam, the Philippines, Malaya, Saigon, Yangon, etc. It was the first time for Taiwan province to participate in the National Games. The projects included men’s athletics, swimming, weight lifting, boxing, wrestling, basketball, volleyball, soccer, table tennis, tennis and softball and women’s athletics, swimming, wrestling, basketball, volleyball, table tennis, tennis and softball.

尺寸 /Size:
Φ33mm×3mm
重量 /Weight:
17g
年代 /Date:
1948

上海
国术比赛大会
纪念章

Commemorative medal of Shanghai Martial Arts Competition

□ 纪念章外沿由多个小三角围成一圈，如同一个放射的太阳，内部镶有蓝色珐琅，刻有“上海国术比赛大会”字样，中心是一个紧握的拳头图案，象征着国术运动员的力量与坚持。

□ 1929 年末到 1930 年初，为解决南方灾民过冬资金以及给慈善机构筹集善款，由李景林带头，黄金荣、杜月笙、张啸林等发起了全国武术擂台大赛，比赛地点定在上海。1929 年 12 月 18 日，上海国术比赛大会在租界亚尔培路（今陕西南路）逸园开幕。这次比赛的奖金惊人，前 12 名选手的奖金共为 13 000 块大洋，第一名奖 3 000 块大洋，第 12 名也能获得 500 块大洋。1930 年 1 月 7 日，擂台赛落下帷幕。曹晏海、马承智、张熙堂获得前三名，三人代表所有获奖选手，将 13 000 块大洋的奖金全部捐献给灾民以及慈善机构。

□ The medal surrounded by several small triangles is like a burning sun, inlaid with blue enamel inside and engraved with the words “Shanghai Martial Arts Carnival”. The center of the medal is a pattern of a tight fist, symbolizing the strength and persistence of Chinese martial arts athletes.

□ From the end of 1929 to the beginning of 1930, in order to raise funds for the disaster-stricken to see the winter out in the south and funds for charities, Li Jinglin took the lead, with the engagement of Huang Jinrong, Du Yuesheng, Zhang Xiaolin and others, to launch the national martial arts carnival in Shanghai. On December 18, 1929, Shanghai Martial Arts Carnival was opened at Canidrome on Avenue du Roi Albert (now West Shaanxi Road). The prize for this competition was amazing. The top 12 players would win 13,000 silver dollars in total, with the first place winning 3,000 silver dollars and the 12th winning 500 silver dollars. After a dozen days of battle, on January 7, 1930, the arena carnival came to an end. Cao Yanhai, Ma Chengzhi and Zhang Xitang won the top three places. On behalf of all the winners, the three donated all the 13,000 silver dollars to the disaster-stricken and charities.

尺寸 /Size：
Φ40mm × 1mm
重量 /Weight：
11.9g
年代 /Date：
1929—1930

第二展厅

EXHIBITION HALL II

奥运之光

OLYMPIC GLORY OF SHANGHAI

第二展厅

EXHIBITION HALL II

经过漫长的历史演变，
奥林匹克运动会成为规模最大、
范围最广、
水平最高的世界体育盛会。
它是现代文明的罕见杰作，
影响力远远超出体育的范畴，
不同肤色、不同语言、不同国家、
不同社会制度、不同宗教信仰、
不同生活习惯的人们，
借此表达着共同的向往。
在中国驶向奥林匹克的漫漫航程上，
上海有着极其特殊的意义。
翻开城市的历史，不难发现，
中国奥运出使之船，
正是从上海启航，走向世界。

After a long historical evolution,
the Olympic Games
have become the world's largest sports
event with the widest scope and
the highest level.
It is a rare masterpiece of
modern civilization, and its influence
goes far beyond sports.
People of different colors,
speaking different languages,
coming from different countries
and different social systems,
having different religious beliefs and
different living habits express their
common yearning
through the Olympics.
Shanghai has played an extremely special role
in China's long voyage to the Olympics.
As we review the history of the city of Shanghai,
it is not difficult to find that China's
ship to the Olympic Games
set sail from Shanghai to the world.

第三十一届夏季奥运会赛用同款自行车头盔（钟天使）
2016 年　巴西里约热内卢
张栋良捐
Bicycle helmet as same as the one used by Zhong Tianshi at the 31st Summer Olympics
2016 Rio de Janeiro, Brazil
Donated by Zhang Dongliang
头盔大胆地使用了国粹京剧之中的"脸谱"作为主题，钟天使的头盔
花木兰脸谱为主要元素，侧面饰有祥云纹样。
he helmet boldly uses the "facial makeup" from Beijing opera, the quintessence
Chinese culture, as the theme. The helmet worn by Zhong Tianshi takes the
makeup of Hua Mulan as the main element, decorated with auspicious cloud patterns
both sides.

古代奥运会纪念币

Commemorative copper coin from the ancient Olympics

□ The father of Alexander the Great of Macedonia, Philip II of Macedon, specially made commemorative copper coins to celebrate his remarkable achievements at the ancient Olympic Games held in ancient Greece. The front face is decorated in high relief with images of ancient Greek Apollo (Olympian god of the sun and light), and the back face is carved with a knight pattern. This is a precious coin for the ancient Olympic Games, which spans 23 centuries. It is the ancestor of the memorial coins of the modern Olympic Games.

□ 这是马其顿亚历山大大帝之父腓力二世为庆贺其在古希腊举办的古代奥林匹克运动会上取得骄人战绩而特别制作的纪念铜币。铜币正面为高浮雕古希腊阿波罗（太阳神）头像，背面雕有骑士图案。这是跨越 23 个世纪的古代奥运会珍贵钱币，堪称奥运会纪念币之鼻祖。

尺寸 /Size：
Φ18mm × 4mm
重量 /Weight：
5.9g
年代 /Date：
公元前 359—公元前 336 年
/359B.C.—336B.C.

奥林匹克圣火采集雕塑

Olympic Flame Lighting Sculpture

第二展厅

EXHIBITION HALL II

□ 雕塑为奥林匹克女祭司采集圣火的形象，采用蜡膜工艺，由纯铜铸造而成，制作工艺精湛、细腻。整座雕塑神态祥和，女祭司五官精致，身材匀称、高挑，身穿根据考古发掘出的雕塑和壁画而创作的古希腊传统服装。女祭司高举燃烧着的圣火盆，庄严而神圣。

□ 奥林匹克圣火是奥林匹克精神的最高象征，代表希望和梦想，光明与欢乐，友谊、和平、平等以及奥林匹克精神所倡导的坚韧不拔、奋斗为乐的价值理念。早在古代奥运会上，持火炬赛跑就是希腊人祭祀仪式的一个不可或缺的项目。1934年，国际奥委会雅典会议决定，恢复古代奥运会的圣火采集仪式。圣火通常于奥运会开幕前几个月在奥运会的发源地——希腊奥林匹亚的赫拉神庙前点燃。圣火点燃后，火种置于一个古老的火盆中，由首席女祭司带到古代奥运会场内的祭坛，点燃第一名火炬手手中的火炬，随后开始前往奥运会主办城市。

□ The sculpture is the torch-igniting ceremony of the high priestess of Olympics. It is made of pure copper by wax modeling process, and it is exquisite and delicate. The whole sculpture is peaceful. The priestess is of well-crafted build and height with delicate facial features. She wears ancient traditional Greek costumes created according to the sculptures and murals unearthed from archaeological discovery. The priestess raises the burning holy flame, solemn and sacred.

□ The Olympic holy flame is the supreme symbol of the Olympic spirit, representing hope and dreams, brightness and joy as well as friendship, peace, equality, and the perseverance and struggle of the values advocated by the Olympic spirit. As early as the ancient Olympic Games, the race with torch in hand was an indispensable project for the sacrifice ceremony of Greeks. In 1934, the Athens Conference of IOC decided to resume the holy flame ceremony of the ancient Olympic Games. The holy flame is usually ignited a few months before the opening of the Olympic Games in front of the Heraion of Samos in Olympia, Greece, the origin of the Olympic Games. After the holy flame is ignited, the flame will be placed in an ancient fire basin. The chief priestess takes the flame to the altar in the coliseum of the ancient Olympic Games, and she ignites the torch held by the first torchbearer, then the torch will be relayed to the host city.

尺寸 /Size:
210mm × 210mm × 610mm
重量 /Weight:
8 100g
年代 /Date:
当代 /Contemporary

第一届
夏季奥运会
赫拉女神纪念牌

Commemorative plaque of the Goddess Hera, the 1st Summer Olympics

□ 这是第一届现代奥运会上颁发的纪念牌，用于纪念本届奥运会。纪念牌正面刻有赫拉女神头像，背面刻有战车驰骋及长翅膀的胜利女神下凡给冠军戴上桂冠的图案。

□ 战车比赛是公元前680年第二十五届古代奥运会上的竞赛项目，依车的类型分为骡车（四轮铬车赛）和驷马战车比赛，此外还有裸骑（无马鞍）赛马等。优胜者将获得神圣的橄榄枝桂冠和“奥林匹克胜利者”银币、战车、马匹、橄榄油等。

□ This is a commemorative plaque issued at the first modern Olympic Games to commemorate the current Olympic Games. The front of the plate is engraved with the head of the goddess Hera, and the back is engraved with the pattern of the goddess of victory, the chariot galloping and the goddess with wings coming down to earth to put the laurel crown on the champion.

□ The chariot competition is a competition sport at the 25th ancient Olympic Games in 680 BC. According to the type of chariot, it was divided into mule chariot (four-wheeled chariot race) and horse chariot race, in addition to naked riding (bareback) horse racing etc. The winners would get a sacred laurel crown made of olive branches and silver coins for “Olympic Winner”, chariots, horses and olive oil.

尺寸 /Size：
Φ35mm × 5mm
重量 /Weight：
24.8g
年代 /Date：
1896

第一届夏季奥运会邮票

Stamps, the 1st Summer Olympics

□ 这套邮票由希腊艺术家吉利隆负责设计、E·穆雄负责雕刻制版，由法国巴黎国家印刷厂印制。邮票全套 12 枚，分正方、横长方及竖长方三种票形，总面值 19.63 德拉马克。

□ 邮票有著名雕塑掷铁饼者、伯拉克西特列斯的《赫尔墨斯》、古希腊拳击、战车赛、古雅典竞技场、胜利女神与古希腊体育运动有关的艺术作品等八种图案，边框装饰富有古希腊的艺术色彩。这是世界上第一套体育邮票，堪称是见证现代奥运会开创的历史文物，被收藏人士誉为“奥运活化石”。

□ The Greek artist Gileron was responsible for the design this set of stamps, and E.Moucmon was responsible for the engraving and it was printed by the National Printing Factory in Paris, France. It is made of carved version with 12 stamps, which are divided into three types: square, transverse rectangle and vertical rectangle, with a total value of 19.63 GRD.

□ This set of stamps includes eight patterns, such as famous sculptures Discobolus, Hermes of Praxiteles, ancient Greek boxing, chariot racing, ancient Athenian arena, Winged Victory of Samothrace and artworks related to ancient Greek sports. The border decoration of stamps is also rich in the artistic color of ancient Greece. This is the first set of sports stamps in the world, which can be called as a historical relic witnessing the founding of the modern Olympic Games. It is praised as “living fossil of Olympics” by collectors.

尺寸 /Size:
205mm × 140mm
年代 /Date:
1896

第一届
夏季奥运会
海报《自行车比赛》
Poster *Cycling*, the 1st Summer Olympics

□ 这幅海报为法国《小日报》的绘图报道，绘有自行车运动员通过终点，接受人群欢呼的场景。为首的自行车运动员身着法国国旗配色的绶带，右手扶车，左手与一名身穿礼服的绅士相握，像是在接受绅士的道贺。海报下方写有法语“在雅典奥运会上，我们的同胞马松，获得单车比赛的冠军”。

□ 保罗・马松（Paul Masson，1874—1944），法国自行车冠军。在 1896 年雅典奥运会上，获自行车场地计时赛、争先赛 10 公里的金牌。

□ This poster is a graphic report by the French *Le Petit Daily*, which depicts the scene of cyclists passing the finish line and receiving cheers from the crowd. The leading cyclist was wearing a sash in the color of the French flag, holding the bicycle with his right hand, and holding a gentleman in a dress with his left hand, an if he was accepting this gentleman's congratulations. Below the poster reads in French "JEUX OLYMPIQUES A ATHÈNES Notre compatriot Masson, vaiqueur de la course vélocipédique".

□ Paul Masson (1874-1944), a French cycling champion. At the 1896 Athens Olympics, he won the gold medal in the cycling track time trial and the 10 kilometer race.

尺寸 /Size：
250mm × 450mm
年代 /Date：
1896

JEUX OLYMPIQUES A ATHÈNES

re compatriote Masson, vainqueur de la course vélocipédique

第二届
夏季奥运会
（世博会）证书
Certificate, the 2nd Summer Olympics (World Expo)

证书是法国艺术大师绘画及雕刻的作品，画面犹如一幅精美的西欧名画，证书上写有法语的“世界博览会”字样。

为借用世界博览会来扩大奥林匹克运动会的影响力，在“现代奥林匹克之父”顾拜旦的努力下，1900 年巴黎奥运会与世博会同期召开。奥运会于 5 月 20 日至 10 月 28 日陆续进行，历时 5 个多月。本届奥运会以“国际体育锻炼和运动竞赛”为名义，将比赛项目按博览会工业类别分在 16 个区域进行。例如，击剑被安排在刀剑制造工业区，划船安排在救生系统展览区等。由此，可以说本届奥运会成为本届世博会的一部分。

Painted and carved by French artist, the picture is like a beautiful and famous Western European painting. The certificate reads “World EXPO” in French.

In order to use the World EXPO to expand the influence of the Olympic sports, under the efforts of Coubertin, the “father of the modern Olympics”, the 1900 Paris Olympic Games was held at the same time as the World EXPO. The Olympic Games was held successively from May 20 to October 28, which lasted for more than five months. In the name of “international physical exercise and sports competition”. the Olympic Games will be divided into 16 regions according to the industrial category of the EXPO. For example, fencing was arranged in the sword manufacturing industry area, boating was arranged in the life-saving system exhibition area, etc. Therefore, it can be said that this Olympic Games has become a part of this World EXPO.

尺寸 /Size:
910mm × 745mm
年代 /Date:
1900

第二届夏季奥运会游泳金牌

Gold medal in swimming, the 2nd Summer Olympics

□ 金牌原为1900年巴黎世博会巴黎造币厂参展作品。由于1900年世博会与奥运会同期召开，金牌被颁发给奥运会游泳比赛冠军澳大利亚运动员弗雷德里克·莱恩。金牌为法国艺术家达尼埃尔－迪皮伊所作，正面为时间女神在云端上手持书卷的场景，边上为一个小天使帮助扶持书卷，书卷上写有“1900”字样。背面为身着双翅的小天使一手擎火炬，一手持一枚银币站立，身后是一台螺旋式压铸机，右侧为称量银子的天秤和币胚，左侧为支架上的币章雕模，周边刻有法文“巴黎造币厂”。

□ 弗雷德里克·莱恩（1880—1969）是第一个为澳大利亚赢得奥运游泳冠军的运动员，1985年入选澳大利亚体育名人堂。他曾效力于英国布莱克普游泳俱乐部和东悉尼业余游泳俱乐部。第二届巴黎奥运会设有200米、1 000米、4 000米自由泳和4×50米自由泳接力、200米仰泳、200米障碍泳、潜泳七个项目的比赛，莱恩获得200米障碍泳和200米自由泳金牌。

□ The gold medal was originally a work exhibited by the Paris Mint at the1900 Paris World Expo. Since the 1900 World Expo was held at the same time with the Olympic Games, the gold medal was awarded to Olympic swimming champion Frederick Lane from Australia. The gold medal was made by French artist Daniel Dupuis. The front is the scene of the goddess of time holding the scroll on the cloud, and a little angel helps support the scroll on the side. The word “1900” is written on the scroll. On the back is a little angel with two wings holding a torch in one hand and a silver coin in the other, with a screw die casting machine behind it, and the coin stamp on the right side of the bracket, with the French “Paris Manufacture” engraved around it.

□ Frederick Lane (1880–1969), Australian, is the first swimming athlete to win the gold medal in the Olympic Games for Australia. He was selected for the Sport Australia Hall of Fame Awards in 1985. He once worked for Blackpool Swimming Club in Britain and East Sydney Amateur Swimming Club. The Paris 1900 Olympic Games set seven swimming events including the 200-meter, 1,000-meter and 4,000-meter freestyle, 4×50-meter freestyle relay, 200-meter backstroke, 200-meter obstacle and underwater swimming. Lane won gold medals for the 200-meter obstacle and 200-meter freestyle swimming.

尺寸 /Size：
Φ50mm × 3mm
重量 /Weight：
34.6g
年代 /Date：
1900

第七届
夏季奥运会
跳水银牌

Silver medal in diving, the 7th Summer Olympics

□ 银牌一面是一位手持橄榄枝与棕榈叶的运动员，其后有肩生双翼的女神虚影，意味着和平及胜利，下方写有“第七届奥林匹克运动会”的字样。背面是为纪念名叫巴拉沃的勇士而设立的安特卫普纪念碑，背景是安特卫普大教堂和港口，顶部刻有“ANVERS MCMXX”字样，意为安特卫普 1920。银牌为美国运动员克拉伦斯·平克斯顿所得。

□ 克拉伦斯·平克斯顿(1900—1961)，美国著名跳水运动员。曾获得第七届安特卫普奥运会男子 10 米台跳水金牌、3 米板跳水银牌；第八届巴黎奥运会 10 米台跳水和 3 米板跳水铜牌。

□ One side of the gold medal is engraved with an athlete holding olive branches and palm leaves, followed by the shadow of a double-winged goddess, symbolizing peace and victory. On the back is the Antwerp monument to a warrior named Balavo, with the Antwerp Cathedral and port in the background, with the inscription “ANVERS MCMXX” on the top, which means Antwerp 1920. The silver medal is for American athlete Clarence Pinkston.

□ Clarennce Pinkston (1900–1961) is a famous American diver. He won the gold medal of Men’s Diving 10m Platform and silver medal of Men’s Diving 3m Springboard in the Antwerp 1916 Olympic Games; the bronze medal of Men’s Diving 10m Platform and Men’s Diving 3m Springboard in the Paris 1924 Summer Olympics.

尺寸 /Size:
Φ60mm × 3mm
重量 /Weight:
53.4g
年代 /Date:
1920

第五届远东运动会奖章

Medals from the 5th Far Eastern Championship Games

□ 这是第五届远东运动会奖章，奖章中间錾刻有举办地中国地标建筑“天坛”的形象，两端是第五届远东运动会的英文名称（FIFTH FAR EASTERN CHAMPIONSHIP GAMES），正下方是举办地、时间（SHANGHAI 1921）。

□ 远东运动会由远东体育协会（原称远东奥委会）主办，是菲律宾、中国、日本等国选手参加的洲际综合性运动会。1921年5月30日至6月4日，第五届远东运动会在上海虹口娱乐场举办，国际奥委会委员、日本体育协会会长加纳治五郎（1909年国际奥委会第10次全会上当选）代表国际奥委会在开幕式上致辞，并向远东体育协会通报国际奥委会在安特卫普（时译为盎凡尔）举行全会的情况。中国选手获运动会总锦标第二，其中篮球、足球、排球夺得冠军。中国田径选手杜荣棠脱颖而出，夺得5项全能和铁饼冠军，袁庆祥获得跳高锦标。6月4日，在四川路基督教青年会举行发奖仪式和闭幕式，除大会奖品外，还有各中外机关团体捐赠的银杯、银瓶、锦旗、铜牌坊、银天坛、油画、银盾、银鼎等33件。

□ This is the medals from the 5th Far Eastern Championship Games. The image of Temple of Heaven, a landmark of China, is engraved in the middle of the medals. At the two ends of the medal is the English name “FIFTH FAR EASTERN CHAMPIONSHIP GAMES”, under which is the place and time (SHANGHAI 1921) of the event.

□ The Far Eastern Championship Games was hosted by the Far Eastern Athletic Association (formerly known as Far Eastern Olympic Committee), which was an intercontinental comprehensive sports event attended by athletes from the Philippines, China, Japan, etc. From May 30 to June 4, 1921, the 5th Far Eastern Championship Games was held at Hongkew Recreational Ground, Shanghai. Jigoro Kano, the IOC Member and President of Japan Sports Association (elected at the 10th General Assembly of IOC in 1909) delivered a speech on behalf of the IOC at the opening ceremony and delivered information on the IOC's General Assembly in Antwerp. China ranked second in the general championship and Chinese athletes won the champion in basketball, soccer and volleyball. Chinese athletics player Du Rongtang stood out, winning champions in pentathlon and discus. Yuan Qingxiang won the champion in the high jump. On June 4, the awarding ceremony and closing ceremony were held at the YMCA on Sichuan Road. In addition to the prizes of the General Assembly, there were also a total of 33 silver cups, silver bottles, brocade flags, bronze archways, silver Temple of Heaven, oil paintings, silver shield and silver cauldron, donated by various Chinese and foreign institutions.

尺寸 /Size：
Φ32mm × 2mm
重量 /Weight：
12.6g
年代 /Date：
1921

尺寸 /Size：
Φ32mm × 2mm
重量 /Weight：
10.9g
年代 /Date：
1921

第八届远东运动会纪念章

Commemorative medal from the 8th Far Eastern Championship Games

□ 这是第八届远东运动会纪念章，纪念章呈长方形，首尾皆呈波浪状，两侧饰以橄榄枝纹样，中间刻有“第八届远东运动大会”字样。

□ 1927 年 8 月 27 日至 9 月 3 日，第八届远东运动会在上海中华运动场（亦称中华棒球场）举行，由中华全国体育协进会具体筹办。当时会员国已发展到 6 个国家，即中国、日本、菲律宾及暹罗、马来亚、印度。其中，中、日、菲共派出 504 名选手参赛。运动会比赛项目设足球、网球、排球、篮球、棒球、游泳、田径和全能运动。另设女子排球、女子网球和乒乓球等表演项目，中国获总锦标赛第二。中国运动员林宝华和邱飞海等一举囊括网球项目单、双打及团体冠军，首次为中国夺得网球项目锦标。

□ This is the Commemorative medal of the 8th Far East Games. The medal is rectangular in shape with waves at the beginning and the end. The two sides are decorated with patterns of olive branches, and the words "The 8th Far East Games" are engraved in the middle.

□ From August 27 to September 3, 1927, the 8th Far Eastern Championship Games was held at the Shanghai China Stadium (also known as the Chinese Baseball Court). It was specially arranged by China National Amateur Athletic Federation. At that time, there were six member states, i.e. China, Japan, the Philippines, Siam, Malaya and India. A total of 504 contestants were sent for the games by China, Japan and the Philippines. The competition sports included soccer, tennis, volleyball, basketball, baseball, swimming, athletics, as well as pentathlon. Demonstration sports including women's volleyball, women's tennis and table tennis were set. China won second place in the general championship. Chinese athletes including Lin Baohua and Qiu Feihai won the champions of tennis single, double and team, which was the first championship of tennis for China.

尺寸 /Size:
27mm × 43mm × 2mm
重量 /Weight:
18.4g
年代 /Date:
1927

《第十届世界运动会报告》

Report on the 10th Summer Olympics

□ 1932 年 7 月 30 日至 8 月 14 日，第十届世界运动会（夏季奥林匹克运动会）在美国洛杉矶举行。中国首次派出了以中华全国体育协进会总干事沈嗣良为团长的代表团。本书为沈嗣良回国后撰写的总结报告，图文并茂，刊名由王正廷所题，前有张伯苓的题词：“智力竞新、强国之鉴”。全书分为：世界运动会史话、世界运动会行政概况、第十届世界运动会地点之决定、第十届世界运动会筹备情形、中国参加第十届世界运动会之动机及成绩、第十届世界运动会概要（参加国名、开幕礼、比赛节目、大会比赛成绩、闭幕礼、杂记、招待情形）、国际田径赛协会会议记等。附录印有塔夫脱记事原文、世界运动会历届优胜运动员表。本书详细描述了 1932 年第十届洛杉矶奥运会期间举办的各种活动，各项比赛情况、奖牌获得者及名称，奖牌样式、证书及举办奥林匹克展览的精彩内容和大量事实图片。其中有近四十幅非常珍贵的图片。不仅有王正廷、张伯苓的照片，还有奥运会创始人顾拜旦的照片，以及洛杉矶奥运会的一些比赛照片。书中收录了一张刘长春与中国代表团成员在奥运会主体育场跑道上举旗前进的全景照片，这是近代中国第一次参加奥运会的珍贵史料。

□ The Tenth World Games (Summer Olympic Games) was held in Los Angeles, United States, from 30 July to 14 August 1932. For the first time, China sent a delegation headed by Wm.Z.L.Sung, Director-General of the All-China Federation of Sports Associations. This book is a summary report written by Wm.Z.L.Sung after returning to China. It is written in a picturesque manner. The title of this book was proposed by C.T.Wang. Before that, there is Chang Po-ling's inscription: "Striving for innovation in competition and learning lessons from powerful countries." The book is divided into: History of World Games, Overview of World Games administration, Decision on the Place of the Tenth World Games, Preparations for the Tenth World Games, Motivations and Achievements of China in the Tenth World Games, Summary of the Tenth World Games (Name of Participating Countries, Opening Ceremony, Competition Program, Achievements of the General Assembly, Closing Ceremony, Monument, Reception), International Athletics Association Conference, etc. Appended with the original text of the Taft's note and the list of winners of the World Games. It depicted in details the various events held during the 10th Los Angeles Olympic Games in 1932, the competitions, medal winners and the titles, styles of medals, certificates and the wonderful content and a large number of factual pictures of the Olympic exhibition. There are nearly 40 very precious pictures. There are not only photos of C.T.Wang and Chang Po-ling, but also photos of the founder of the Olympic Games, Pierre de Coubertin, and some games of the Los Angeles Olympic Games. The memorial contains a panoramic photo of Liu Changchun and members of the Chinese delegation holding a flag on the main stadium runway of the Olympic Games. This is the precious historical material for China's first time to participate in the Olympic Games in modern times.

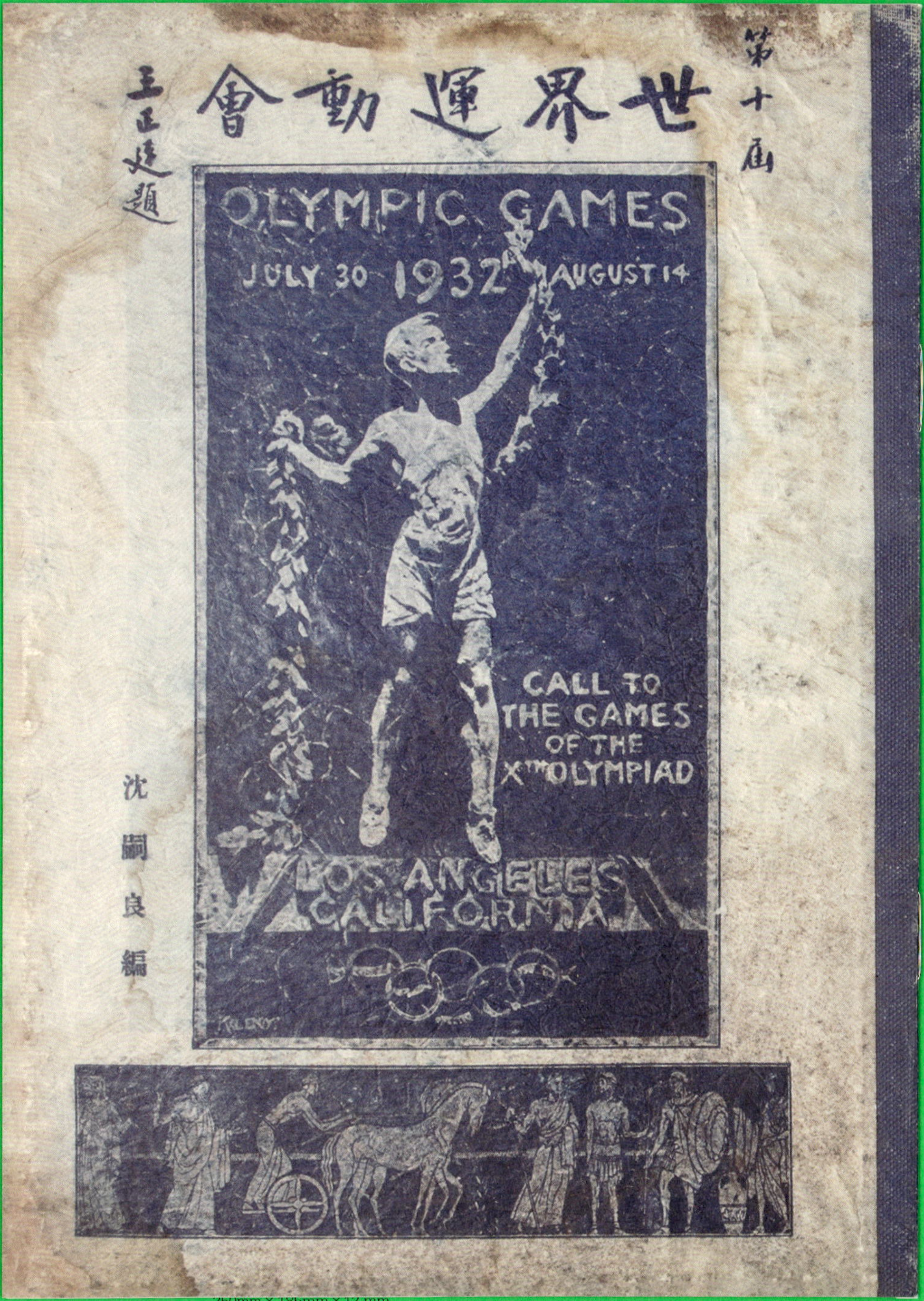

250mm × 185mm × 12 mm
年代 /Date：
1933

《第十届奥运会（洛杉矶 1932）官方报告》

10th Olympiad Los Angeles 1932 Official Report

□ 1932 年 7 月 30 日至 8 月 14 日，第十届夏季奥林匹克运动会在美国洛杉矶举行。共有来自 37 个国家的 1 408 名运动员参加了洛杉矶奥运会，中国和哥伦比亚为首次参加奥运会。开幕式上，按照国家的英文字母顺序，中国代表团第 8 个入场，刘长春手擎国旗在前，后为代表团团长沈嗣良，再后是教练宋君复。由于代表团人数太少，当时在美国春田学院留学的东吴大学毕业生刘雪松、赴美观摩奥运会的时任上海交通大学体育主任韩国侨民申国权与在美休假的上海西侨青年会体育主任美国人托平（亦称托屏）加入中国代表团的队伍当中，与宋君复走在一排。旧金山总领事黄亦苏及其夫人坐在主席团上。刘长春原拟参加 3 个短跑项目，因旅途劳顿，体力不支，放弃了 400 米跑，仅参加了 100 米、200 米短跑。比赛开始后，由于准备不足，仓促上阵，刘长春未能发挥出自己的水平，百米预赛成绩在 11 秒 1，居小组第五位，被淘汰；200 米成绩 22 秒 1，居小组第四位，也被淘汰。虽中国第一次参加奥运会的比赛成绩不佳，但“盖此代表四万万人之一人，在美国及世界运动会，实认为富有价值之收获也”，“其将以此为微小之起点，以逐渐发扬光大之，使中国人特殊之精神与能力，尽量表显于全世界乎”。

□ 作为奥运会最权威的官方出版物，这本官方报告制作宏大，精美厚重，包含了从第十届奥运会准备阶段到奥运会结束的所有资料，包括运动员成绩，代表团信息、门票详细信息（类别、发行量等）、比赛情况、奖牌获得者及名称、奖牌样式、证书及举办奥林匹克展览的精彩内容和大量事实图片。第 396 页刊登有刘长春参加比赛的大幅照片及他参加的 100 米、200 米比赛成绩等，第 397 页图片下的文字说明为：THE LONE REPRESENTATIVE OF FOUR HUNDRED MILLION PEOPLE（四万万中国人的唯一代表）。第 342 页中有中国代表团入场式照片，这些都是中国首次参加奥运会的珍贵图文史料。

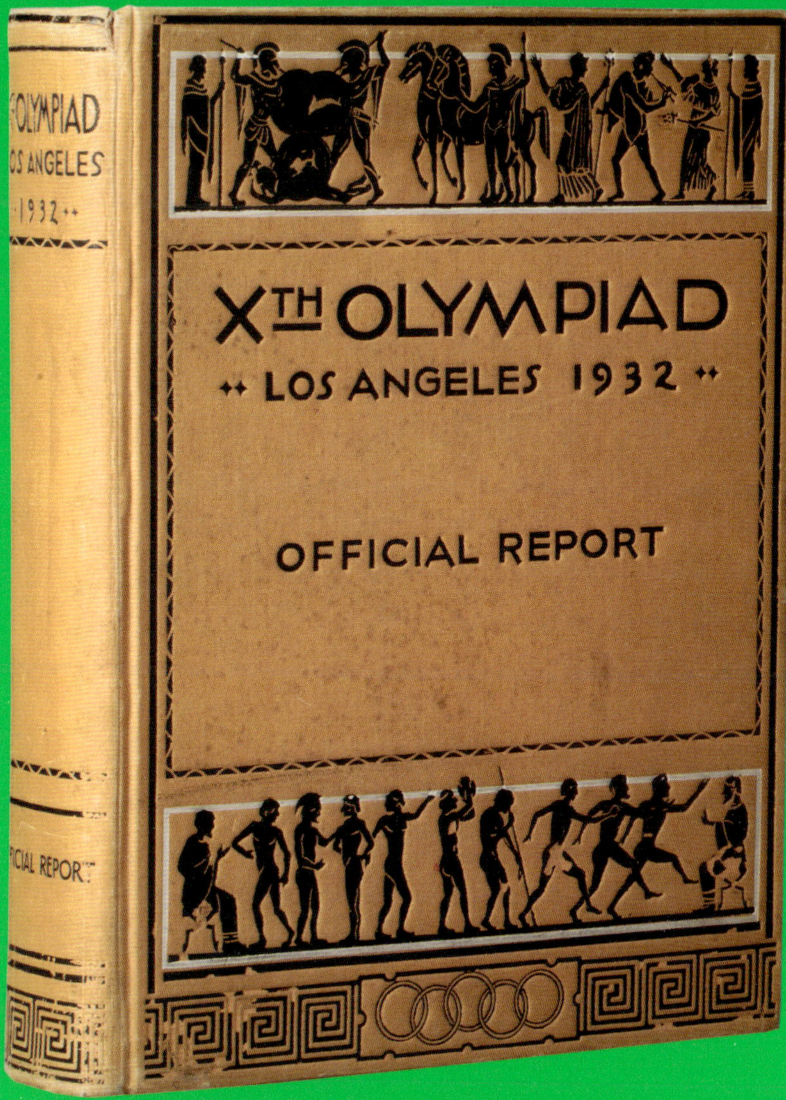

作者 /Compiled：
第十届夏季奥运会组委会编
Edited by the Organizing Committee of the 10th Summer Olympic Games
尺寸 /Size：
240mm × 310mm × 58mm
年代 /Date：
1932

第十一届夏季奥运会号码布

Bib number, the 11th Summer Olympics

□ This is the number cloth of Chinese race walker Zhou Yuyu who once participated in the 11th Berlin Olympic Games in 1936, the number is "112".

□ In 1936, Zhou Yuyu won the "award for beautiful walking posture" in the Berlin Olympic Games, and won the first Olympic medal for China. Zhou Yuyu has developed his whole life to the cause of the Chinese Olympic Games. In 1992, Zhou Yuyu went to Beijing to participate in the activity of bidding for Olympic Games of 2000 despite his age.

□ 这是中国竞走运动员周余愚参加1936年第十一届柏林夏季奥运会时的号码布，编号为“112”号。

□ 1936年，周余愚在柏林奥运会中获得“最佳姿势优美奖”，为中国夺得第一块奥运奖牌。周余愚一生心系中国奥运事业，1992年，周余愚不顾年迈之躯，赴京参加2000年申奥活动，助力北京申奥。

尺寸 /Size:
300mm × 200mm
捐赠者 /Donated by:
周明辉 /Zhou Minghui
年代 /Date:
1936

老式相机

Vintage camera

□ 这是铅球运动员陈宝球携带至 1936 年第十一届奥运会赛场上的相机。

□ 陈宝球 (1910—1937)，原籍广东南海，出生于上海。著名田径运动员，曾求学于上海大夏大学，为校体育健将。因身高力大，人称“铁牛”。20 世纪 30 年代，加入上海白虹田径队，并成为主力队员。1935 年，在民国第六届全运会上陈宝球以 13.26 米打破男子铅球全国纪录，同年入选中国体育代表团；1936 年，赴柏林参加第十一届奥林匹克运动会男子铅球比赛。参赛期间，用陈宝球这台照相机记录下了许多珍贵的奥运影像和故事。

□ This is the vintage camera carried by shot-put player Chen Baoqiu to the 11th Olympic Games in 1936.

□ Chen Baoqiu (1910–1937), originally from Nanhai, Guangdong province, was born in Shanghai. He was a famous athlete of athletics who once studied at the Great China University in Shanghai, serving as a master sportsman of the school. He was called the “irony bull” because of his height and strength. In the 1930s, he joined in Shanghai Baihong Athletics Team and became the leading player of the team. In 1935, at the 6th National Games of the Republic of China, Chen Baoqiu broke the national record of men’s shot-put with a length of 13.26 meters and was selected as a Chinese sports delegation in the same year. In 1936, he went to Berlin to participate in the men’s shot-put competition of the 11th Olympic Games. During the competitions, Chen Baoqiu recorded many precious scenes and stories about Olympic Games with this camera.

尺寸 /Size:
140mm × 60mm × 100mm
捐赠者 /Donated by:
陈圣造 /Chen Shengzao
年代 /Date:
1930s

第十一届夏季奥运会大型铜铃

Big brass bell from the 11th Summer Olympics

□ This is a big brass bell used in athletics competitions of the 11th Berlin Summer Olympics. One face of the bell is engraved with the national emblem pattern of Berlin Olympic Games — the Prussian Eagle and five-ring mark of the Olympics; the other face is engraved with the words “die XI olympischen sommerspiele in berlin 1936”.

□ The competition-used bell is generally used as the reminder of the athletics competition, preliminary of swimming competition or the last circle. This bell is used for timing of athletics competitions.

□ 这是第十一届柏林夏季奥运会田径比赛使用的大型铜铃。铃铛外壁一面刻有柏林奥运会的会徽——普鲁士鹰和奥运五环的结合。另一面则刻有德文“1936 年第十一届柏林奥运会”字样。

□ 赛用铜铃一般用于田径、游泳比赛预备或最后一圈距离时的提醒示意，此铜铃为田径比赛计时用。

尺寸 /Size:
Φ142mm × 345mm
重量 /Weight:
878.8g
年代 /Date:
1936

第十一届
夏季奥运会
铜制镀银纪念钱袋

Silver-plated bronze commemorative purse from the 11th Summer Olympics

A all-metal-made chain mail pocket, with a diameter of 6.8cm when opened, and was presented to Mr. Wm.Z.L.Wang's wife as a gift for a distinguished lady by IOC.

这是国际奥委会赠予贵宾夫人的礼物，由沈嗣良先生的夫人收藏。钱袋由全金属制链甲组成，打开时直径 6.8 厘米，开口上刻有奥运五环的图案。

尺寸 /Size：
Φ40mm × 100mm
重量 /Weight：
56.1g
捐赠者 /Donated by：
蒋世琦 /Jiang Shiqi
年代 /Date：
1936

罗马
ROME
1956
MELBOURNE
1952
赫尔辛基
HELSINKI

1980 莫斯科 MOSCOW
1984 洛杉矶 LOS ANGELES
1988 汉城 SEOUL
1992 巴塞罗那 BARCELONA
1996 亚特兰大 ATLANTA
2000 悉尼 SYDNEY
2004 雅典 ATHENS
2008 北京 BEIJING
2012 伦敦 LONDON
2016 里约热内卢

第十一届夏季奥运会火炬

Torch of the 11th Summer Olympics

☐ 1936 年第十一届柏林奥运会是现代奥运会火炬传递的开始。7 月 20 日，柏林奥运会圣火在奥林匹亚点燃，希腊人康斯但丁成为现代奥林匹克火炬接力历史上的第一位火炬手。

☐ 火炬由卡尔·迪姆设计，弗里德里希·克虏伯·许特韦克制作。火炬整体呈银色，由经抛光处理的钢材料制成，燃料采用金属镁。手柄部分刻有“奥林匹亚火炬接力－柏林 1936”的文字，字体上方有奥林匹克五环旗和德国的鹰徽标志，下方则镌刻本次火炬传递的路线图，火炬顶部的平台上还写有“感谢火炬手”的字样。

☐ The 1936 11th Berlin Olympic Games marked the beginning of the torch relay in modern Olympics. On July 20, Berlin Olympic Flame was lighted in Olympia. A Greek named Constantine became the first torchbearer in the history of modern Olympic torch relays.

☐ Designed by Cal Dem and made by Friedrich Krupp AG, the torch is silver in its entirety and made of polished steel material with magnesium metal fuel. The handle bears the inscription of “fackelstaffel-lauf olympia-berlin 1936” (in German meaning “Olympic Torch relay Berlin 1936”), above which are the Olympic Rings flag and German eagle emblem and below which is the inscription of the route map of the torch relay. The platform on the top of the torch is inscribed with the text to express thanks to the torchbearers.

尺寸 /Size:

Φ155mm × 270mm

重量 /Weight:

460g

年代 /Date:

1936

第十四届夏季奥运会火炬

Torch of the 14th Summer Olympics

□ 火炬通体由金属制成，分为火盘和手柄两部分。火盘上写有“第十四届奥运会伦敦 1948”字样，上部镂空有奥运五环图案，火炬整体造型简约、古朴。本届奥运会圣火的燃料是镁，燃烧效果更好，即使在阳光明媚时也能看清楚火焰的形状。

□ 本届奥运会火炬接力活动历时 12 天，途经 7 个欧洲国家，全长 3 365 公里。这是在二战后的第一次奥林匹克盛会，整个奥运圣火接力都以“和平”为主题，在从奥林匹亚到伦敦的接力过程中，举行了很多体现和平象征的活动。

□ Made of metal in its entirety, the torch is composed of two parts: the fire bowl and the handle. Embossed “XIVth Olympiad 1948 Olympia to London” with pierced Olympic Rings in the upper part, the overall shape of the torch is simple and antique. The fuel for the Olympic flame is magnesium, which has better combustion effects, making the shape of the flame clearly visible even in the bright sunshine.

□ The Olympic torch relay lasted 12 days and travelled 7 countries in Europe, covering a distance of 3,365 kilometers. It was the first Olympic gathering after the Second World War. With “peace” as the theme for the whole Olympic Flame relay, many activities reflecting symbols of peace were held in the relay from Olympia to London.

尺寸 /Size:
Φ145mm × 470mm
重量 /Weight:
960g
年代 /Date:
1948

第十五届夏季奥运会火炬（复制品）

Torch of the 15th Summer Olympics (Replica)

□ 火炬头部呈圆锥形，上面写有“第十五届奥运会赫尔辛基 1952”字样，下面则用英文和芬兰文写有“赫尔辛基”字样。在火炬头的中部，绘有一个装饰性的月桂树枝，而另一面上画有奥林匹克五环标志。火炬的手柄部分由木料制成，并涂了漆。

□ 本次奥运会首次动用飞机将火种从雅典空运到丹麦，经哥本哈根运送到赫尔辛基，时间是 1952 年 7 月 19 日。从丹麦经瑞典到达芬兰的路程采用了跑步、骑马、自行车和独木舟等传递方式。火炬接力历时 25 天，由 3 372 名火炬手完成传递活动。

□ The torch head is conical, inscribed with “XV OLYMPIA HELSINKI 1952” in the upper part and “HELSINKI” in English and Finnish in the lower part. A decorative laurel wreath is painted in the middle of the torch head and the Olympic Rings are painted on the other side. The handle of the torch is partly made of wood in a coat of paint.

□ The Olympic Games resorted to an airplane to ship the fire from Athens to Denmark, which was delivered to Helsinki via Copenhagen on July 19, 1952. Such ways as running, horse riding, bicycles and canoes were adopted in the journey from Denmark to Finland via Sweden. The torch relay lasted 25 days and the handover was completed by 3,372 torchbearers.

尺寸 /Size：
128mm × 547mm
重量 /Weight：
600g
年代 /Date：
1952

第十六届夏季奥运会火炬

Torch of the 16th Summer Olympics

□ 火炬由火盘和手柄两部分组成，外观呈银色，由铝制作而成，在杯状火炬头下部，有奥林匹克五环标志和“第十六届奥运会墨尔本 1956”字样。

□ 墨尔本奥运会圣火由350名火炬手从奥林匹亚传递到雅典。沿途设计了一些有特色的活动，如在雅典的卫城两名战士身着战装在传递路线上挡住火炬手的路，只有当火炬手说“圣火是我从奥林匹亚带来的”才允许通过。墨尔本奥运会火炬接力是当时奥运史上行程最长的火炬接力活动。

□ Composed of a fire bowl and a handle, the torch is made of aluminium in a silver appearance. Below the cup-like torch head are the Olympic Rings and “MELBOURNE: XVI OLYMPIAD 1956”.

□ The Melbourne Olympic Flame was relayed from Olympia to Athens by 350 torchbearers. Some characteristic activities were devised on the way. For instance, the way of the torchbearer was barred by two soldiers in the uniform of warriors in the acropolises in Greece. He was only allowed to enter when he said “I am bringing the Flame of Olympia”. The torch relay for the Melbourne Olympic Games covered the longest distance in the Olympic history by that time.

尺寸 /Size：
Φ150mm × 400mm
重量 /Weight：
960g
年代 /Date：
1956

第十七届
夏季奥运会
火炬

Torch of the 17th Summer Olympics

□ 火炬由阿梅迪奥・马伊里设计，采用了古典风格，下部有“第十七届奥运会”字样。火炬材质首次采用铜铝合金，燃料开始使用比较清洁的丙烷。

□ 奥运圣火在奥林匹亚点燃，先由希腊的火炬接力手传至雅典，经由海路送到意大利的西西里岛，途经意大利各地，最后到达罗马。本届奥运圣火传递共有 1 529 名火炬手参与，行程 2 750 公里。本届奥运会首次对火炬接力进行了电视转播，这一做法也使得更多的人可以目睹圣火的风采。

□ Designed by Amedeo Maiuri, the torch adopted a design in the classical style with “XVII Olympiad” in its lower part. The torch uses bronzed aluminum for its material for the first time and starts to use propane, a cleaner substance, for its fuel.

□ Lighted in Olympia, the Olympic Flame was first carried to Athens by Greek torchbearers and delivered to Italy’s Sicily by sea before reaching Rome via different places in Italy. The Olympic Flame relay was participated by 1,529 torchbearers in total and covered a distance of 2,750 kilometers. The Olympic Games aired the torch relay by television, a practice allowing more people to witness the mien of the Flame.

尺寸 /Size：
Φ150mm × 400mm
重量 /Weight：
580g
年代 /Date：
1960

第十八届夏季奥运会火炬

Torch of the 18th Summer Olympics

□ 火炬呈圆柱状，用不锈钢和铝制成。造型线条刚劲有力，外面覆有不锈钢，里面可填充燃料。为减轻火炬整体的重量，托盘部分特用铝材料制成。火炬上有“第十八届奥运会东京 1964”字样以及奥林匹克五环标志。

□ 东京奥运会圣火火种通过飞机运载前往日本，前后通过航运、陆地和海运方式共经过了 26 065 公里，火炬接力参与人数达到 100 603 人，在奥运会火炬接力参与人数上创下了纪录。

□ The torch is made of stainless steel and aluminium in a cylindrical shape. Clad with stainless steel inside which the fuel can be filled, it features a vigorous and powerful figure. To reduce the entire weight of the torch, the bowl is partly made of special aluminium. The torch is inscribed with “XVIII Olympiad Tokyo 1964” and Olympic Rings.

□ The fire of the Tokyo Olympic Flame was shipped to Japan by airplane and traveled a total distance of 26,065 kilometers by air, land and sea successively with 100,603 participants in the torch relay, hitting a record in terms of the number of participants in the Olympic torch relay.

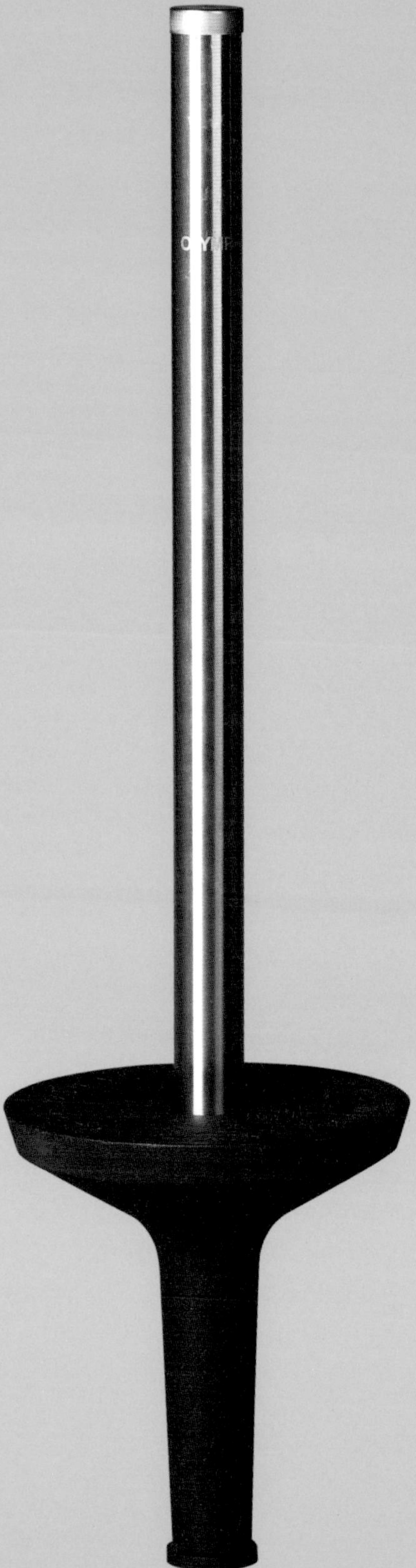

尺寸 /Size：
Φ170mm × 648mm
重量 /Weight：
826g
年代 /Date：
1964

第十九届夏季奥运会火炬

Torch of the 19th Summer Olympics

□ 火炬由一把主火炬和两把副火炬组成。主火炬呈圆锥形，顶部带有与本届奥运会会徽和宣传画上同样的“Mexico 68”字样，并采用了开槽通透的设计。两款副火炬外形相似，均为圆锥形，手柄部分为木质，火炬上方饰有象征和平的白鸽，手柄下方有“墨西哥”字样。两款副火炬的不同之处在于，一款是由黑色金属制作，而另一款则是由银色金属制作。

□ 墨西哥城奥运会火炬接力的主题是“新大陆”。为此圣火运送到伟大航海家哥伦布的诞生地意大利热那亚市。圣火穿越大西洋，沿着哥伦布发现新大陆的路线航行。本届奥运会第一次使用彩色电视技术向全世界转播。为了加强裁判员的责任感，开幕式上首次列入裁判宣誓。

□ The torches are composed of one major torch and two minor ones. The major torch is conical in an engrooved design, inscribed with “Mexico 68” on the top, the same text as those on the emblem and the poster of the Olympic Games. The two minor torches are both conical in similar shapes. The handles are made of wood. The top of the torches is decorated with doves as a symbol of peace and the handle is inscribed with “Mexico” in the lower part. The difference between the two minor torches lies in the manufacture of one with black metal and that of the other with silver metal.

□ The theme of the torch relay for the Mexico City Olympic Games is “The Relay to the New World.” To this end the flame was shipped to Genoa, Italy, birthplace of Columbus, a great voyager. The flame crossed the Atlantic Ocean and sailed along the route leading to Columbus’ discovery of the New World. The Olympic Games applied the technology of color television to air it to the whole world. The opening ceremony included the oath-taking of the referees to strengthen their sense of responsibility.

副火炬 /Minor torch
尺寸 /Size:
Φ110mm × 530mm
重量 /Weight:
792.5g
年代 /Date:
1968

主火炬 /Major torch
尺寸 /Size:
Φ105mm × 460mm
重量 /Weight:
1 200g
年代 /Date:
1968

副火炬 /Minor torch
尺寸 /Size:
Φ110mm × 530mm
重量 /Weight:
706.6g
年代 /Date:
1968

1 2 3

第二十届夏季奥运会火炬

Torch of the 20th Summer Olympics

□ 火炬由克虏伯主持设计，以不锈钢为材料，由手柄、托架和燃烧管三部分组成。火炬的燃烧管外部有“第二十届奥运会慕尼黑 1972”字样，手柄部分的托架上有奥林匹克五环标志和本届大会的会徽，形如四射的光芒。整个火炬造型以传统奥运火炬为范本，再融入当时的流行元素，给人以古典而又不失时代感的视觉享受。

□ 本届奥运会第一次选择了一位女性——田径选手海蒂·舒勒尔宣读奥林匹克誓词。这对全世界的女性运动员来说，无疑是一种巨大的鼓舞。

□ With Krupp presiding its design, the torch uses stainless steel for its material and consists of three parts: the handle, the plate and the fire pipe. The exterior of the fire pipe of the torch is inscribed with “München 1972 Spiele der XX. Olympiade” and the plate of the handle bears the Olympic Rings and the emblem of the Olympic Games shaped like glittering light. The shape of the entire torch follows the models of traditional Olympic torches and integrates the popular elements at that time, contributing to antique but fashionable visual enjoyment.

□ The Olympic Games chose a female—an athletics athlete named Héthy Chouleur—for the first time to read out the Olympic oath. It was undoubtedly a great encouragement for female athletes all over the world.

尺寸 /Size：
Φ210mm × 725mm
重量 /Weight：
1 350g
年代 /Date：
1972

第二十一届夏季奥运会火炬

Torch of the 21st Summer Olympics

□ 火炬以重量较轻的铝制成。火炬的手柄为红色，上面镶嵌着白色的奥运会标志；火炬的头部为钻有许多小孔的黑色圆柱体，将其设计成黑色是为了使火焰在照片上更醒目。为了表示对奥运圣火发源地的崇敬，火炬使用了经特殊处理的橄榄油作为燃料。

□ 开幕式上的火炬最后由一对青年男女运动员点燃，这是奥运会史上的第一次、也是唯一一次由两人共同执行这一光荣的使命。

□ The torch is made of aluminium, a lighter material. The torch has a red handle with an embedded white Olympic logo. The head of the torch is a black cylinder with many small holes. It is designed to be black so as to make the flame more eye-catching in the picture. The torch uses specially processed olive oil for the fuel to show respect for the origin of the Olympic Flame.

□ The torch in thc opcning ceremony ended being lighted by a young male athlete and a young female one. It was the first and only time in the Olympic history that the glorious mission was jointly executed by two persons.

尺寸 /Size：
Φ80mm × 660mm
重量 /Weight：
540g
年代 /Date：
1976

第二十二届夏季奥运会火炬

Torch of the 22nd Summer Olympics

□ 火炬上刻有“莫斯科奥运会 1980”字样，燃烧器周围是一个由同心圆组成的金色杯状托架，托架上有本届奥运会的会徽。火炬燃料由丙烷和丁烷混合而成，燃烧时间长达 8~10 分钟。

□ 本届奥运会火炬接力经过了希腊、保加利亚、罗马尼亚和苏联，共 4 915 公里，5 000 人参与了火炬接力，这是奥林匹克运动会第一次来到社会主义国家。

□ The torch bears the inscription "МОСКВА – ОЛИМПИАДА - 1980." Around the burner is a golden-colored cup-like plate formed of concentric circles with the emblem of the Games on it. The fuel is a mixture of propane and butane for a combustion duration of 8 to 10 minutes.

□ The torch relay of the Games traveled Greece, Bulgaria, Romania and the Soviet Union, covering a total distance of 4,915 kilometers and participated by 5,000 people. This was the first time that the Olympic Games had been to a Socialist country.

尺寸 /Size:
Φ95mm × 570mm
重量 /Weight:
700g
年代 /Date:
1980

第二十三届夏季奥运会火炬

Torch of the 23rd Summer Olympics

□ 火炬主要材质为铝合金及铜合金，手柄部分用皮革制成，并套有金光闪闪的环状金属装饰物，以丙烷作燃料。火炬上有“第二十三届奥运会洛杉矶 1984”和用拉丁语蚀刻的奥林匹克格言“更快、更高、更强”字样，以及大会主体育场的纪念塔图案，整个火炬设计庄重、古朴。

□ 1984 年奥运会火炬接力历时 83 天，穿越 33 个州，到达美国 41 个城市，全程 19 000 公里。此届奥运会是中国重返国际奥委会后首次派代表团参加的夏季奥运会，并获得 15 枚金牌，许海峰成为中国第一位奥运会冠军。

□ The main material for the torch is bronze tinted aluminium. The handle is partly made of leather with a glittering decorative metal band. The fuel is propane. The torch bears the caption of “Games of the XXIII Olympiad Los Angeles 1984” and the Olympic motto etched in ancient Latin, Citius Altius Fortius (Faster, Higher, Stronger), along with the graphic of the Los Angeles Memorial Coliseum. The design of the entire torch is solemn and antique.

□ The torch relay for the 1984 Olympic Games lasted 83 days, crossed 33 states and reached 41 cities in the United States of America, covering a distance of 19,000 kilometers. The Olympic Games was the first one that the People’s Republic of China had sent its delegation to take part in. China won 15 gold medals and Xu Haifeng became the first Olympic champion in China.

尺寸 /Size：

Φ120mm × 580mm

重量 /Weight：

1 200g

年代 /Date：

1984

第二十四届夏季奥运会火炬

Torch of the 24th Summer Olympics

□ 火炬以铜为主要材料，手柄部分裹有皮革。火炬头部写有“第二十四届奥运会汉城 1988”字样，并装饰有本届奥运会会徽，上面还雕刻着龙纹图案，寓意着东西方的和谐。

□ 1988 年汉城奥运会火炬接力被认为是一次“伟大的火炬接力”。火炬接力活动体现了韩国的传统文化，传递路线是一个连接韩国东西部之间的“Z”形路线，体现了阴阳两极的平衡统一。火种由飞机从雅典运往韩国济州岛，整个接力活动历时 26 天，20 899 人参与接力，行程 15 250 公里。

□ The torch uses bronze for its main material and the handle is covered by leather. The torch head bears the inscription of "Games of the XXIV Olympiad Seoul 1988" and is decorated with the emblem of the Games. It is also engraved with dragons, symbolizing the harmony of East and West. The torch relay for the 1988 Seoul Olympic Games was considered to be a "great torch relay".

□ The torch relay reflected the traditional Korean culture, following a Z-shaped route connecting the east and the west of the Republic of Korea, symbolizing the balanced unity of yin and yang. The fire was shipped by airplane from Athens to Chejudo of the Republic of Korea. The entire relay lasted 26 days and was participated by 20,899 people, covering a distance of 15,250 kilometers.

尺寸 /Size：

Φ105mm × 510mm

重量 /Weight：

1 000g

年代 /Date：

1988

第二十五届夏季奥运会火炬

Torch of the 25th Summer Olympics

□ 火炬由铝制成，主体为银色，外表呈流线型。火炬手柄部分写有“第二十五届奥运会巴塞罗那 1992”字样，并装饰有本届奥运会的会徽。在火炬的设计中出现的圆锥形和三角形是受到了双耳细颈的椭圆土罐和拉丁帆的启发，具有典型的地中海特征。

□ 奥运会主火炬的点火方式是现代奥运史上一个难以被超越的经典。来自西班牙的残疾射箭运动员雷波洛用箭接过火炬上的火种后，在巴塞罗那的夜空中射向 70 米远处、高 21 米的圣火台，主火炬被点燃的一瞬间，全世界为之欢呼。本届奥运会上，上海运动员庄泳、杨文意分别夺得了女子 100 米自由泳冠军和女子 50 米自由泳冠军。

□ The torch is made of aluminium, the torch features a silver main body in a streamlining appearance. The handle of the torch bears the inscription of "XXV Olimpiada Barcelona 1992" and is decorated with the emblem of the Olympic Games. The conical and triangular shapes that appear in the design of the torch are inspired by the amphora and by the Latin sail, giving it a typical Mediterranean character.

□ The major torch of the Olympic Games was lighted in a classical way difficult to be emulated in the modern Olympic history. A Spanish Paralympic archer named Rebollo took over the fire of the torch and shot an arrow to the torch tower 70 meters apart and 21 meters high in the night sky of Barcelona. The moment when the major torch was ignited, the whole world applauded. In the Olympic Games, Zhuang Yong and Yang Wenyi, athletes from Shanghai, respectively won the championships for the women's 100-meter freestyle swimming competition and the women's 50-meter freestyle swimming competition.

尺寸 /Size：
Φ180mm × 680mm
重量 /Weight：
1 200g
年代 /Date：
1992

第二十六届
夏季奥运会
火炬

Torch of the 26th Summer Olympics

□ 火炬由一束直管组成，外边套有金属环。火炬的外形象征了古希腊建筑的线条，充满了古典气息。火炬身上的 22 根铝管代表着历史上曾举办过的二十二届夏季奥林匹克运动会，在上边的镀金铜环上有“亚特兰大 1996”字样和本届奥运会的会徽，而在下边的环上写着所有举办过现代奥运会的城市名字。这把火炬是历届夏季奥运会火炬中最长的一把，也是迄今唯一一把需要手握中间部位的火炬。火炬的底部由五环和阿拉伯数字 100 构成，纪念奥运会已经走过百年历史；而火炬的上半部由火焰变成的星星，则象征每一位运动员的卓越追求。

□ 上海游泳运动员乐靖宜在本届奥运会上夺得100米自由泳的金牌，并打破奥运会纪录，在中国奥运史上留下了光辉的一笔。

□ The torch is composed of a bunch of reeds surrounded by metal bands. Being fully classical, the shape of the torch symbolizes the lines of classical Greek architecture. The 22 aluminium reeds of the torch represent the 22 Summer Olympic Games held in history. The upper golden bronze band bears the inscription of "Atlanta 1996" and the emblem of the Olympic Games and the lower band is inscribed with the names of all the cities where the modern Olympic Games were held. The torch has been the longest one among the torches for all the Summer Olympic Games and the only one to date that needs to be gripped in the middle. The bottom of the torch consists of the Rings and the Arabian numeral of 100 in memory of the centenary of the Olympic Games. The stars changed from the flame in the upper part of the torch symbolize the transcendent pursuit of each athlete.

□ Le Jingyi, a swimming athlete from Shanghai, won a gold medal in the 100-meter freestyle swimming competition in the Olympic Games and broke the Olympic record, leaving a shining mark in the Chinese Olympic history.

尺寸 /Size:
Φ65mm × 800mm
重量 /Weight:
1 600g
年代 /Date:
1996

第二十七届夏季奥运会火炬

Torch of the 27th Summer Olympics

□ 火炬分为三层，分别象征着土、火和水。内层由不锈钢制成，里面盛有燃料系统和燃烧系统；中层由蓝色电镀铝制成，用以盛放燃料罐；铝制外层包裹着其余两层。火炬的设计理念来自悉尼歌剧院的建筑轮廓、太平洋蔚蓝的海水以及“飞去来器”精妙的弧线，整个火炬的造型则像澳大利亚土著人用的飞镖。燃料使用丙烷和丁烷的混合物。

□ 悉尼奥运会的火炬传递途经十三个国家，共有 13 300 名火炬手参加，历时 127 天，传递距离达 27 000 公里。在圣火传递中，完成了奥运史上首次进行水下火炬传递。在本届奥运会上，上海运动员陶璐娜、王励勤分别夺得女子 10 米气手枪冠军和乒乓球男双冠军，用自己的实力为国人争得了荣誉。

□ The torch has three layers that respectively symbolize earth, fire and water. The inside layer is made of stainless steel and contains the fuel system and the combustion system. The middle layer is made of blue anodized aluminium and contains the fuel reservoir. The outer aluminium layer enwraps the other two. The design idea originates from the architectural contour of the Sydney Opera House, the blue of the Pacific Ocean and the delicate arch of the boomerang. The shape of the entire torch is like the dart used by the Australian aboriginals. The fuel is a mixture of propane and butane.

□ Participated by 13,300 torchbearers, the torch relay for the Sydney Olympic Games traveled 13 countries and lasted 127 days, covering a distance of 27,000 kilometers. In the relay of the Flame, the first underwater torch relay in the Olympic history was completed. In the Olympic Games, Tao Luna and Wang Liqin, athletes from Shanghai, respectively won the championships of the women's 10-meter air pistol competition and the table tennis men's doubles, winning honors for the Chinese with their own abilities.

尺寸 /Size：
Φ110mm × 770mm
重量 /Weight：
1 000g
年代 /Date：
2000

第二十八届
夏季奥运会
火炬
Torch of the 28th Summer Olympics

□ 火炬由希腊著名设计师安德雷亚斯・瓦罗佐斯设计而成，外观设计呈橄榄叶状，线条流畅、协调，由金银两色的金属和木质手把构成，这种设计使火炬燃烧时呈现出喷薄向上的动感。设计师融入了“万物适中”的设计理念，火炬外形简洁美观。超前并富有活力的设计，充分突出了奥运火焰的神圣感。

□ 本次奥运会火炬首次传遍了全世界的五大洲，历时 78 天，经过全球 35 个城市后，回到雅典。在本届奥运会比赛中，上海运动员吴敏霞夺得女子双人跳水 3 米板冠军；上海运动员刘翔以 12.91 秒的成绩追平了由英国选手科林・杰克逊创造的世界纪录，夺得冠军，为中国奥运史增添了新的荣耀。

□ Designed by Andreas Varotsos, a famous Greek designer, the exterior of the torch is shaped like an olive tree leaf with smooth and harmonious lines and golden and silver metal and wooden handles. The design enables the torch to reveal a spurting dynamic when the torch burns. The designer integrates the philosophy of "Everything in Moderation" and makes the torch in a simplistic and beautiful shape. The unprecedented and vibrant design fully highlights the sacredness of the Olympic flame.

□ The Olympic torch spread the Five Continents in the world for the first time and lasted 78 days before it returned to Athens via 35 cities in the globe. In the Olympic Games, Wu Minxia, an athlete from Shanghai, won the championship in the women's double 3-metre springboard diving competition; Liu Xiang, an athlete from Shanghai, equalized the world record for 12.91 seconds made by a British athlete named Colin Jackson and won the championship, adding new glory to the Chinese Olympic history.

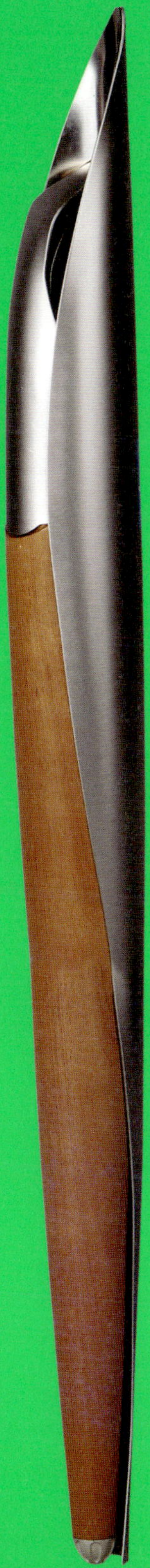

尺寸 /Size：
Φ60mm × 680mm
重量 /Weight：
700g
年代 /Date：
2004

第二十九届夏季奥运会火炬

Torch of the 29th Summer Olympics

□ 火炬设计理念来自“渊源共生，和谐共融”的“祥云”图案。火炬造型的设计灵感来自中国传统的纸卷轴。源于汉代的漆红色的运用使之明显区别于往届奥运会火炬设计，红银对比的色彩产生醒目的视觉效果。上下比例均匀分割，祥云图案和立体浮雕式的工艺设计使整个火炬高雅华丽、内涵厚重。 在工艺方面使用锥体曲面异型一次成型技术和铝材腐蚀、着色技术。

□ 北京奥运会火炬接力历时 130 天，总里程约 13.7 万公里，参与传递火炬手 21 780 人，是迄今为止线路最长、范围最广、参与人数最多的一次奥运圣火传递。上海运动员在本届奥运会中获得了五枚金牌，其中吴敏霞第二次夺得女子双人跳水 3 米板奥运会金牌；王励勤夺得乒乓球男子团体金牌；刘子歌在女子 200 米蝶泳比赛中获得金牌，并打破了世界纪录；火亮夺得男子双人 10 米台跳台金牌；邹市明获得男子拳击轻量级金牌。

□ The design philosophy originated from the auspicious clouds graphic signifying "Same Origin, Good Harmony". The design of the shape of the torch is inspired by the traditional Chinese parchment scroll. The use of the Chinese lacquer red originated from the Han Dynasty evidently differs from the designs of the torches for previous Olympic Games and the contrasting colors of red and silver create an eye-catching visual effect. The upper part and the lower part are evenly proportional and the lucky clouds graphic and the technological design of plastic relief make the entire torch elegant and beautiful with profound implications. It applies the one-time cone surface molding technology and aluminium corrosion and coloring technology.

□ The torch relay for the Beijing Olympic Games lasted 130 days, covering a total distance of about 137,000 kilometers and participated by 21,780 torchbearers. It has been the Olympic Flame relay with the longest route, the most extensive coverage and the most participants. The athletes from Shanghai won 5 gold medals in this Olympic Games. Among them, Wu Minxia won an Olympic gold medal in the women's double 3-metre springboard diving competition for a second time; Wang Liqin won a gold medal for the table tennis men's team competition; Liu Zige won a gold medal and broke the world record in the women's 200-meter butterfly swimming competition; Huo Liang won a gold medal in the men's double 10-meter platform diving competition; Zou Shiming won a gold medal in the men's lightweight boxing competition.

尺寸 /Size:
Φ76mm×720mm
重量 /Weight:
985g
年代 /Date:
2008

第三十届夏季奥运会火炬

Torch of the 30th Summer Olympics

□ 火炬由爱德华·巴伯和杰·奥斯格比设计，名为“Barberosgerby”，这是史上最轻的奥运火炬。其形状为三棱形，象征了奥运会“更高、更快、更强”的口号。金色的铝合金外表面镂刻有象征 8 000 个火炬接力手的 8 000 个圆孔，这是奥运史上第一次将人的元素加入到火炬中，也充分表明了伦敦奥运会的创新性。

□ 2012 年伦敦奥运会火炬传递全程 3 000 公里，历经 34 个城市，有 500 名火炬手参与。本届奥运会上，上海运动员吴敏霞一举夺得女子双人跳水 3 米板和女子单人跳水 3 米板两枚金牌；上海运动员徐莉佳夺得中国帆船史上在激光雷迪尔级中的首枚奥运金牌；邹市明卫冕男子拳击轻量级冠军。

□ Designed by Edward Barber and Jay Osgerby, the torch is named “Barberosgerby.” It has been the lightest Olympic torch in history. The triangular shape of the torch symbolizes the Olympic motto of citius, altius, fortius (Faster, Higher, Stronger). The golden envelope made of aluminium alloy is perforated by 8,000 circles in reference to the 8,000 torchbearers. It was the first time in the Olympic history that a human element had been added to the torch, fully showcasing the innovation of the London Olympic Games.

□ The torch relay for the 2012 London Olympic Games covered a total distance of 3,000 kilometers via 34 cities and was participated by 500 torchbearers. In the Olympic Games, Wu Minxia, an athlete from Shanghai, won two gold medals respectively in the synchronized diving 3-meter springboard women and the women's individual 3-meter springboard diving competition; Xu Lijia, an athlete from Shanghai, won the first Olympic gold medal in the Laser Radial class in the Chinese sailboat history; Zou Shiming retained his championship in the men's lightweight boxing competition.

尺寸 /Size:
100mm × 64mm × 800mm
重量 /Weight:
800g
年代 /Date:
2012

第三十一届夏季奥运会火炬

Torch of the 31st Summer Olympics

□ 炬身为白色，由再生铝和树脂材料打造而成。火炬在传递时会展示出五条明亮的波形起伏的金属色带。每一层色带的颜色都象征了巴西的自然景观：底部一环深色对应着科帕卡巴纳海滩上著名的波纹形黑白相间的人行道景观，上面两层蓝色涟漪代表了海洋，往上是绿林环绕的山峦，最顶层金黄意味着阳光和金牌，同时这五种颜色还对应着巴西国旗的颜色。

□ 里约奥运火炬途经 300 多个城市，传递距离长达 2 800 公里，1.2 万名火炬手参与了圣火传递。本届奥运会上，上海运动员吴敏霞获得女子双人跳水 3 米板冠军，这是她的第五枚奥运金牌；上海运动员钟天使获场地自行车女子团体竞速赛冠军，实现了中国自行车队奥运金牌零的突破；上海运动员许昕凭借出色的表现，夺得乒乓球男团冠军。

□ The body of the torch is white and made of recycled aluminium and resin. The torch reveals five bright metal segments in a floating effect in the relay. The color of each layer symbolizes Brazil's natural landscape: The dark color ring at the bottom corresponds to the famous corrugated black-and-white sidewalk landscape on the beach of Kopakabana. The two layers of blue strontium above it represent the sea, and the upper layer represents the mountain covered by green forests. The top layer of golden color means the sun and gold medal, and the five colors also correspond to the color of the Brazilian national flag.

□ The torch relay of Rio Olympics passed through more than 300 cities, covering a distance up to 2,800 km. 12,000 torchbearers participated in the relay of holy fire. At this Games, Wu Minxia, an athlete from Shanghai, won the championship of 3-meter springboard in women's synchronized diving, which is her fifth Olympic gold medal; Zhong Tianshi, also an athlete from Shanghai, won the championship of women's team racing in track cycling, making a breakthrough in winning gold medals for the Chinese cycling team; Xu Xin, another athlete from Shanghai, clinched the gold medal of men's team in table tennis with his excellent performance.

尺寸 /Size：
Φ90mm × 780mm
重量 /Weight：
1 500g
年代 /Date：
2016

第三十二届夏季奥运会火炬

Torch of the 32nd Summer Olympics

第二展厅

EXHIBITION HALL II

□ 火炬由日本设计大师吉冈德仁设计，造型灵感来源于日本的樱花，不仅火炬顶部设计成花瓣状，颜色也呈粉亮的“樱花金”色，奥运火种将从五个“樱花花瓣”处点燃，汇集至中央的“花蕊”部分。火炬主要材质采用铝材，大部分取自于2011年日本大地震时灾区临时住房的建材，象征着希望与和平。制作采用了使用在新干线制造中的铝挤压工艺，该工艺可达到“无缝衔接”的效果。

□ 由于2020年新冠疫情的影响，第三十二届奥运会推迟一年举办。奥运圣火在奥运会发源地古奥林匹亚采集完毕后，直接抵达日本，在日本保存一年，于2021年3月25日在日本福岛县重启圣火接力，圣火巡回全国47个都道府县的859个市区町村。

□ The torch is designed by Japanese famous designer Tokujin Yoshioka. Its shape is inspired from Japanese cherry blossoms. Not only the top of the torch is designed in a cherry-petal shape, but also it adopts a bright "pink-gold" color. The torch will be ignited from five "cherry blossom petals" and the flames will gather in the part of central "stamen". The main body of the torch is made of aluminum most of which is collected from the building materials used for temporary housing in the disaster area during the 2011 Japan Earthquake, which embodies hope and peace. The torch is made through the aluminum extrusion process used in the manufacturing of Shinkansen trains, which can achieve the effect of "seamless connection."

□ The 32nd Olympic Games will be postponed for one year due to the 2020 COVID-19 pandemic. The Olympic holy fire will be directly sent to Japan after being collected in Olympia where the ancient Olympics Games originated, and preserved in Japan for one year. On March 25, 2021, the holy fire relay was restarted in Fukushima Prefecture, Japan, and tour 47 prefectures including 859 cities, districts, towns and villages.

尺寸 /Size:
Φ115mm × 710mm
重量 /Weight:
1 200g
年代 /Date:
2020

第十四届冬季奥运会火炬

Torch of the 14th Winter Olympics

□ 火炬由燃烧部和手柄两部分构成，在手柄座处刻有金色“萨拉热窝 84”字样，由世界著名体育用品生产商美津浓采用精钢制作，通体闪耀着金色的光芒。

□ 本届冬奥会火炬于 1 月 29 日从希腊运到南斯拉夫滨海城市杜布罗伏尼克后，采取了与以往不同的传递方式，分南北两路进行火炬接力，最后于波斯尼亚 – 黑塞哥维那会合。点燃主体场火焰的是南斯拉夫花样女子滑冰冠军，21 岁的桑德拉 · 杜布拉夫西奇。而在开幕式上代表运动员和比赛官员宣誓的分别是来自东道主的高山滑雪运动员博扬 · 克里萨伊和高山滑雪裁判员德拉根 · 佩洛维奇。

□ The torch consists of two parts: the combustion part and the handle. The handle base is engraved with words “Sarajevo 84” in gold. It is made of stainless steel by Mizuno, a word-renowned sports good manufacturer, and the whole body shines with golden light.

□ After the torch of this Winter Olympics was transported from Greece to Dubrovnik, a coastal city in Yugoslavia, on January 29, it adopted a different method of transmission from the past, The flame on the main field was lit by Yugoslav women's figure skating champion, 21-year-old Sandra Dubravcic. On behalf of the athletes and race officials, the oaths at the opening ceremony were respectively from the host alpine skier Bojan Krisai and alpine ski judge Dragan Pelovic.

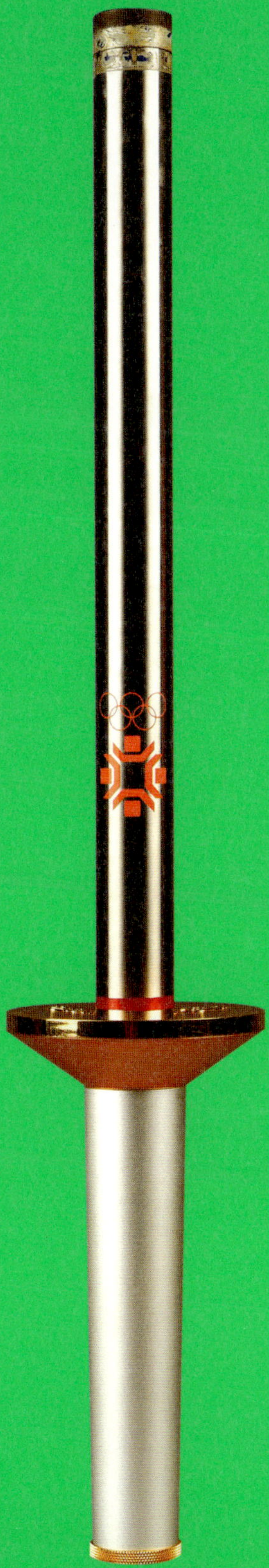

尺寸 /Size:
Φ110mm × 580mm
重量 /Weight:
1 300g
年代 /Date:
1984

第十八届冬季奥运会火炬

Torch of the 18th Winter Olympics

□ 火炬的设计灵感来自过去在日本使用的松枝火把，外形流畅。火炬整体为六边形，代表雪晶体；火炬上部有奥运五环，中间部位镌刻有象征着冰雪项目角逐的冬奥会会徽——“五彩的雪花”，以及“长野 1998”的字样。金黄色的两个流苏缠绕在火炬下方，既隔绝了火炬燃烧时产生的热量，也让整个火炬显得非常具有东方文化特色，是整个火炬的点睛之笔。火炬上面呈金黄色，下面逐渐过渡到银白色，令整个火炬看上去光彩四射。燃料为丙烷。

□ 长野冬奥会的圣火在希腊采集。火炬在东京点燃后，分三路穿越全日本 47 个县。这三路火炬于冬奥会开幕前夕在长野县首府长野市会合。

□ The design of the torch is inspired by the pine torch used in Japan in the past, with smooth shape. The torch is hexagonal in shape, representing snow crystals; on its upper part are Olympic five rings, and its middle part is engraved with “colorful snowflakes” the emblem of Winter Olympic Games symbolizing the competition of ice and snow projects, and the characters “Nagano 1998.” The two golden-yellow tassels are wrapped around the lower part of the torch, which not only isolates the heat generated when the torch is burning but also makes the whole torch extremely distinctive for the eastern cultural features. It is just the striking point of the whole torch. The golden-yellow color on its upper part is gradually changed into silvery-white on its lower part, making the whole torch look bright and radiant. The fuel is propane.

□ The holy fire of Nagano Winter Olympic Games was collected in Greece. After ignited in Tokyo, the torch relay toured 47 prefectures across Japan in three pathways. The torch relay in these three pathways finally converged in Nagano City — the capital of Nagano Prefecture, on the eve of the opening of the Winter Olympic Games.

尺寸 /Size：
Φ123mm × 550mm
重量 /Weight：
1 300g
年代 /Date：
1998

第十九届冬季奥运会火炬

Torch of the 19th Winter Olympics

□ 火炬由萨姆·西尔顿设计，以冰与火为主题，结合了传统和现代元素，数以千计不同尺寸的部位零件，由源自英国和日本的原料制作完成。火炬上方为玻璃花冠，以象征冬奥会的冰山雪景。外观则像一支非常规则的箭，上大下小。

□ 奥运圣火由曾夺得冬奥会冰球金牌的美国国家队 20 位成员点燃，这也是历史上点燃主火炬的人数之最。2002 年盐湖城冬奥会的口号是“点燃心中之火”，冬奥会的激情与活力，也为正处于“9·11”悲痛中的美国人点燃了希望。

□ Designed by Sam Hilton. the torch is a combination of traditional and modern elements, presenting the theme of ice and fire. Its thousands of parts with different sizes are manufactured by raw materials from UK and Japan. The corolla-shaped torch is made of glass, symbolizing icebergs and snow scenes of the Olympic Winter Games. It looks exactly like an arrow, bigger at the upper part and smaller at the lower part.

□ The holy fire of this Games was ignited by 20 members of the United States National Ice Hockey Team who had won the gold medal of Winter Olympic Games. It is the largest number of people in history who ignited the main torch. The slogan of 2002 Salt Lake City Winter Olympic Games was named “Light the Fire within”. The passion and vitality of the Winter Olympic Games also lighted a hope for Americans who were in deep grief caused by the “9·11” terrorist attack.

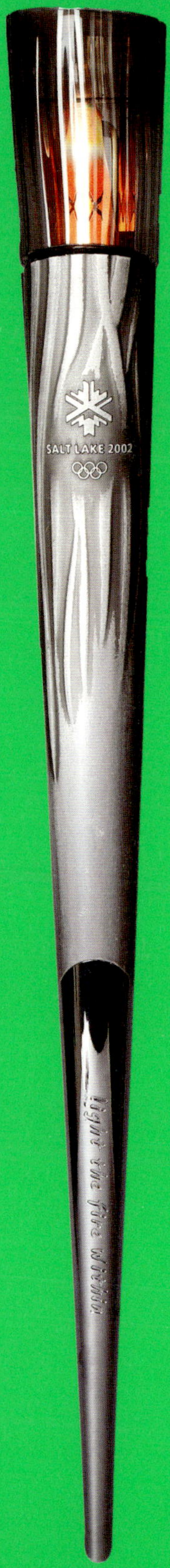

尺寸 /Size：
Φ90mm × 800mm
重量 /Weight：
1 350g
年代 /Date：
2002

第二十届
冬季奥运会
火炬

Torch of the 20th Winter Olympics

☐ 火炬外形似传统的木火把，外表运用了覆盖隔热涂料的铝材，内部则是高科技的钢铜合金。圣火通过火炬顶部的 13 个孔冒出，火焰高度被精准地控制在 10 厘米以下。

☐ 都灵冬奥会圣火在希腊古奥林匹亚被点燃，火炬传递途径 140 多个城市，达到 11 300 公里。本届冬奥会开幕式在都灵奥林匹克体育场举行。开幕式的表演“激情在这里燃烧”充分诠释了奥林匹克精神。

☐ Looking like a traditional wooden one in shape, the external surface of the torch is made of aluminum covered with insulating mold coating, and its internal side is made of high-tech steel and copper alloy. The flame is emitted through 13 holes on the top of the torch, and the height of flame is accurately controlled below 10 cm.

☐ The holy fire of Turin Winter Olympic Games was ignited in Olympia, Greece. The torch relay passed through more than 140 cities, covering a distance up to 11,300 km. The opening ceremony of this Winter Olympic Games was held at the Turin Olympic Stadium. The performance of the opening ceremony — “The passion lives here” fully interpreted the Olympic spirit.

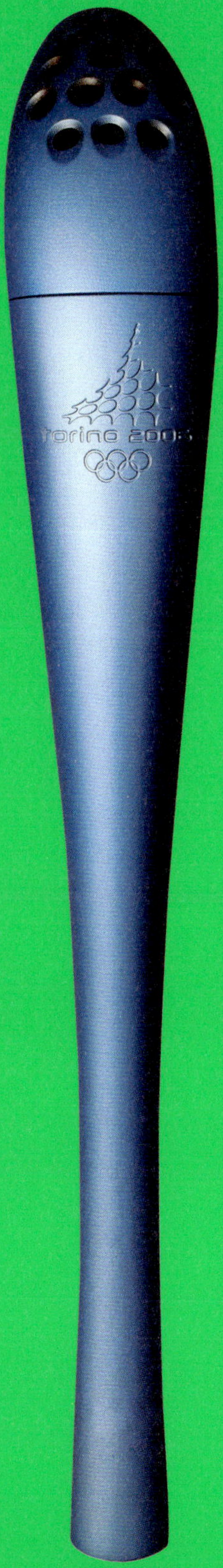

尺寸 /Size:
100mm × 60mm × 760mm
重量 /Weight:
1 850g
年代 /Date:
2006

第二十一届冬季奥运会火炬

Torch of the 21st Winter Olympics

□ 火炬为流线型设计，颜色主要为白色。设计灵感来自于加拿大白雪覆盖的起伏地形和滑雪者冲下雪坡时在雪上留下的滑痕。火炬上镶有冬奥会会徽，还有一个红色的枫叶形开口。枫叶是加拿大的象征，这个枫叶形的开口也是火炬的通风口。

□ 冬奥会火炬传递于 2009 年 10 月 30 日至 2010 年 2 月 12 日举行，为期 106 天，行程 4.5 万公里，传递路程是冬奥会历史上最长的。

□ A streamlined design is applied to the torch whose main color is white. The design is inspired by the undulating terrain covered by snow in Canada and the skiing marks left on snow when skiers rush down the snow slope. The torch is inset with an emblem of Vancouver Winter Olympic Games, and on its top there is a red maple-leaf-shaped opening. Maple leaves are a symbol of Canada, and this maple-leaf-shaped opening is also a vent for the flame.

□ The torch relay of this Olympic Winter Games was started on October 30th, 2009 and ended on February 12th, 2010, lasting for 106 days and covering a distance of 45,000 kilometers. This relay route was the longest one in the history of Winter Olympic Games.

尺寸 /Size：
100mm × 40mm × 950mm
重量 /Weight：
1 600g
年代 /Date：
2010

第二十二届冬季奥运会火炬

Torch of the 22nd Winter Olympics

□ 火炬材质为铝合金，尽管火炬上宽下窄，但设计人员精心考虑了火炬重心位置，非常方便火炬手把持。火炬构造使其能很好地适应俄罗斯严寒和大风天气。设计灵感来源于俄罗斯关于不死火鸟（凤凰涅槃）的神话传说，因此整体造型呈羽毛状，中间镂空，正面和侧面主要为亮银色，后面、镂空处及把手下方带有红色。火炬正面标有冬奥会会徽。

□ 本次火炬传递路线超过 65 000 公里，在 123 天时间里穿越 2 900 多个城镇和居民点。

□ The torch is made of aluminum alloy. Although the torch is wide at the upper part and narrow at the lower part, the designer took the center of gravity into careful consideration for the torchbearer's convenience. The structure of the torch was designed to be well adapted to the weather characteristic of severe cold and gale in Russia. The design is inspired from the Russian mythical legend on the immortal fire bird (Phoenix Nirvana). Therefore, it adopted a feather-like shape, with the inside hollowed out. The main color on the front and side are bright silver, and the back, the hollowed out part and the part below the handle are decorated with red color. The front of the torch is marked with the emblem of Sochi Winter Olympic Games.

□ The torch relay covered a distance beyond 65,000 km, passing through more than 2,900 cities, towns and residential areas in 123 days.

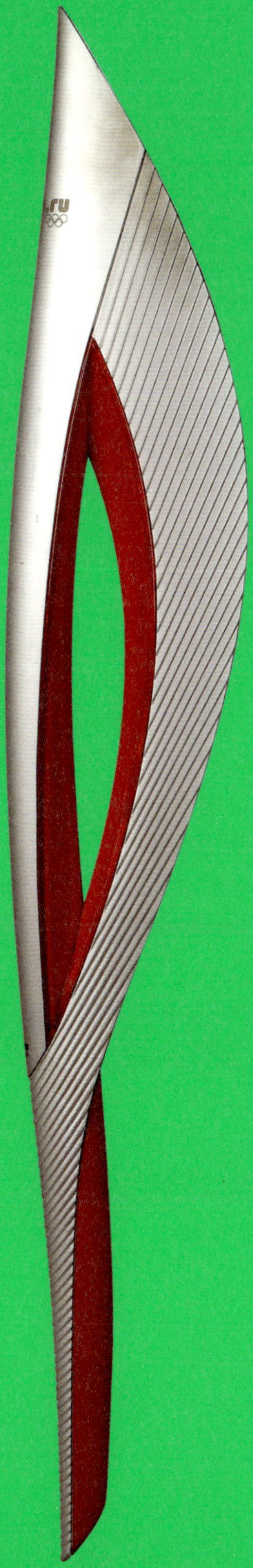

尺寸 /Size：
140mm × 60mm × 950mm
重量 /Weight：
1 800g
年代 /Date：
2014

第二十三届冬季奥运会火炬

Torch of the 23rd Winter Olympics

□ 火炬以白色和金色为主色调，70 厘米的高度代表平昌 700 米的海拔高度。火炬点燃后火焰将向 5 个方向燃烧，这是“☆”——平昌的象征，该符号同时刻在火炬的下半部和顶部周围。

□ 2017 年 10 月 24 日，平昌冬奥会圣火采集仪式在古奥林匹亚举行。此后，平昌冬奥会火炬在希腊境内进行了 8 天的传递后来到韩国境内。本届冬奥会火炬传递历时 109 天，经过 8 005 名火炬手。并且传递方式多样，通过机器人、海底缆车、热气球等方式，展现了韩国科技与文化。

□ The torch is mainly in white and golden colors, with a height of 70cm representing the 700m, altitude of Pyeongchang. After being ignited, the torch will burn in five directions, forming the shape of "☆" — which is the symbol of Pyeongchang. The symbol is carved around both its lower part and its top.

□ On October 24, 2017, the torch collection ceremony for the PyeongChang Winter Olympics was held in Ancient Olympia. Since then, the torch of the PyeongChang Winter Olympics has been relayed in Greece for 8 days and then arrived in Republic of Korea. This Winter Olympics torch relayed lasted 109 days and passed through 8,005 torchbearers. In addition, there are various delivery methods, such as robots, submarines cable cars, hot air balloons, etc., showing Korean technology and culture.

尺寸 /Size：
Φ90mm × 700mm
重量 /Weight：
1 300g
年代 /Date：
2018

奥运会
参与者奖牌

Medals for Participants of Olympics

□ 每届奥运会的参与者奖牌设计独特，独具各国城市特征，集奥运精神与民族风情于一体，精美大气，是历届奥运会另类的缩影。对于奥运的每一位参与者而言，经过了奥运会的历练，能更好地展示自我，同样值得骄傲。每一个参加奥运大家庭聚会的国家和地区都是赢者，每一个来相聚的运动员和志愿者都是胜利者，所以每一届奥运会都为参与者精心设计了参与者奖牌。

□ The medals for participants of different sessions of the Olympics are uniquely designed, which show characteristics of the host cities. Combined with the Olympic Spirit and customs of different ethnic groups, they are exquisite and noble, showing the unique epitome of the Olympics. For every participant of the Olympics, they can better show themselves after the games, which is also something to be proud of. Every country and region participating in the Olympic Games is the winner. Every athlete and volunteer is the winner. Therefore, every session of the Olympics exquisitely designed medals for the participants.

夏季奥运会参与者奖牌

Medals for Participants of Summer Olympics

尺寸 /Size:
Φ50mm×5mm
重量 /Weight:
58.7g
年代 /Date:
1896

国际奥委会全会襟章

Badges for the International Olympic Committee Session

□ 1894 年 6 月 23 日，国际奥委会由法国的教育家皮埃尔・德・顾拜旦男爵发起，在巴黎召开的国际体育代表大会上成立。1894 年成立后，总部设在巴黎。1914 年第一次世界大战爆发，为了避免战火的洗劫，1915 年 4 月 10 日总部迁入有“国际文化城”之称的瑞士洛桑。国际奥林匹克委员会全体会议（简称“国际奥委会全会”）是国际奥林匹克委员会的最高权力机构，奥林匹克运动中一切重大问题的决策权均由全会掌握。从国际奥委会成立至 2022 年 2 月共召开过 139 次全会。

□ 这是国际奥委会委员参加国际奥委会全会时佩戴的襟章，主席和委员的襟章都是唯一的，佩戴的丝带拥有特定的颜色。

□ On June 23, 1894, the IOC was initiated by the French educator Baron Pierre de Coubertin and was founded at the International Athletic Congress in Paris. After its establishment in 1894, it was headquartered in Paris. In 1914, World War I broke out. In order to avoid being destroyed by the war, the headquarters was moved to Lausanne, Switzerland on April 10, 1915, which is known as the “International Cultural City”. The General Assembly of the International Olympic Committee (short as “the IOC Session”) is the highest authority of the IOC, and the decision-making powers of all major issues in the Olympics are held by the IOC Session. A total of 139 sessions were held from its foundation to February 2022.

□ This is the badge worn by the IOC members when they participate in the IOC plenary session. The badges of the chairman and the members are unique, and the ribbons they wear have a specific color.

尺寸 /Size:
27mm × 56mm × 7mm
重量 /Weight:
24.1g
年代 /Date:
1977

尺寸 /Size:
38mm × 60mm × 7mm
重量 /Weight:
44.9g
年代 /Date:
1978

尺寸 /Size:
33mm × 65mm × 10mm
重量 /Weight:
41.7g
年代 /Date:
1980

尺寸 /Size:
30mm × 72mm × 5mm
重量 /Weight:
55.7g
年代 /Date:
1985

尺寸 /Size:
30mm × 60mm × 6mm
重量 /Weight:
28.9g
年代 /Date:
1986

尺寸 /Size:
30mm × 50mm × 6mm
重量 /Weight:
21.7g
年代 /Date:
1988

尺寸 /Size:
35mm × 56mm × 8mm
重量 /Weight:
26g
年代 /Date:
1991

尺寸 /Size:
35mm × 66mm × 8mm
重量 /Weight:
48.6g
年代 /Date:
1993

尺寸 /Size:
35mm × 60mm × 10mm
重量 /Weight:
29.1g
年代 /Date:
1993

尺寸 /Size:
30mm × 70mm × 8mm
重量 /Weight:
22.6g
年代 /Date:
1994

尺寸 /Size:
35mm × 67mm × 6mm
重量 /Weight:
42.1g
年代 /Date:
1995

尺寸 /Size:
50mm × 72mm × 8mm
重量 /Weight:
37.9g
年代 /Date:
1996

尺寸 /Size:
30mm × 57mm × 8mm
重量 /Weight:
34.9g
年代 /Date:
1997

尺寸 /Size:
Φ45mm × 8mm
重量 /Weight:
36.8g
年代 /Date:
1998

尺寸 /Size:
40mm × 50mm × 9mm
重量 /Weight:
16.4g
年代 /Date:
2000

尺寸 /Size:
30mm × 60mm × 6mm
重量 /Weight:
35g
年代 /Date:
2001

尺寸 /Size:
30mm × 50mm × 5mm
重量 /Weight:
10g
年代 /Date:
2002

尺寸 /Size:
30mm × 55mm × 7mm
重量 /Weight:
25.1g
年代 /Date:
2005

尺寸 /Size:
32mm × 34mm × 8mm
重量 /Weight:
14.8g
年代 /Date:
2006

尺寸 /Size:
33mm × 50mm × 16mm
重量 /Weight:
28g
年代 /Date:
2008

奥运会吉祥物

Mascots of the Olympic

□ The mascot of each Olympic Games is an animal or a figure representing the Olympic Games. It takes the Olympic Games as the theme to show the unique geographical characteristics, history and culture of the host city, realize the Olympic spirit, convey the concept of the Olympic Games and publicize the history and culture of the host city, so as to create a festival atmosphere for the Olympic Games.

□ 奥运会吉祥物，是代表各届奥运会的动物或人物，以奥运会作为主题来显示主办城市的独特地理特征、历史和文化，实现奥林匹克精神、传达奥运会概念以及宣传主办城市的历史和文化，为奥运会营造一个节日气氛。

夏季奥运会吉祥物

Mascots of Summer Olympic

第二十届
夏季奥运会吉祥物——猎犬
Mascot for the 20th
Summer Olympics – Waldi
尺寸 /Size：
480mm × 110mm × 200mm
年代 /Date：
1972

第二十二届
夏季奥运会吉祥物——熊
Mascot for the 22nd
Summer Olympics – Misha
尺寸 /Size:
170mm × 140mm × 330mm
年代 /Date:
1980

第二十一届
夏季奥运会吉祥物——海狸
Mascot for the 21st
Summer Olympics – Amik
尺寸 /Size:
300mm × 100mm × 200mm
年代 /Date:
1976

第二十三届
夏季奥运会吉祥物——老鹰
Mascot for the 23rd
Summer Olympics – Sam
尺寸 /Size:
170mm × 110mm × 240mm
年代 /Date:
1984

第二十四届
夏季奥运会吉祥物——老虎
Mascot for the 24th
Summer Olympics – Hodori
尺寸 /Size:
330mm × 125mm × 210mm
年代 /Date:
1988

第二十五届
夏季奥运会吉祥物——卡通狗
Mascot for the 25th
Summer Olympics – Cobi
尺寸 /Size:
340mm × 119mm × 300mm
年代 /Date:
1992

第二十六届
夏季奥运会吉祥物——抽象人物
Mascot for the 26th
Summer Olympics – Izzy
尺寸 /Size:
430mm × 130mm × 310mm
年代 /Date:
1996

第二十七届
夏季奥运会吉祥物——针鼹猬、翠鸟、鸭嘴兽
Mascots for the 27th
Summer Olympics – Millie, Olly, Syd
尺寸 /Size:
170mm × 160mm × 300mm
220mm × 210mm × 280mm
530mm × 180mm × 300mm
年代 /Date:
2000

第二十八届
夏季奥运会吉祥物——妹妹、兄长
Mascots for the 28th
Summer Olympics – Athena, Phevos
尺寸 /Size:
400mm × 105mm × 200mm
年代 /Date:
2004

第二十九届
夏季奥运会吉祥物——福娃
（贝贝、晶晶、迎迎、妮妮、欢欢）
Mascots for the 29th
Summer Olympics – Fuwa
(Beibei, Jingjing, Yingying, Nini,
Huanhuan)
尺寸 /Size:
240mm × 350mm × 150mm
年代 /Date:
2008

第三十届
夏季奥运会吉祥物——钢块
Mascot for the 30th
Summer Olympics – Wenlock
尺寸 /Size:
330mm × 116mm × 265mm
年代 /Date:
2012

第三十二届
夏季奥运会吉祥物——机器人
Mascot for the 32nd
Summer Olympics – Miraitowa
尺寸 /Size:
170mm × 110mm × 260mm
年代 /Date:
2020

第三十一届
夏季奥运会吉祥物——巴西动物
Mascot for the 31st
Summer Olympics – Vinicius
尺寸 /Size:
470mm × 147mm × 270mm
年代 /Date:
2016

冬季奥运会吉祥物

Mascots of Winter Olympic

第十届
冬季奥运会吉祥物——滑雪人
Mascot for the 10th
Winter Olympics – Schuss
尺寸 /Size：
120mm × 54mm × 40mm
年代 /Date：
1968

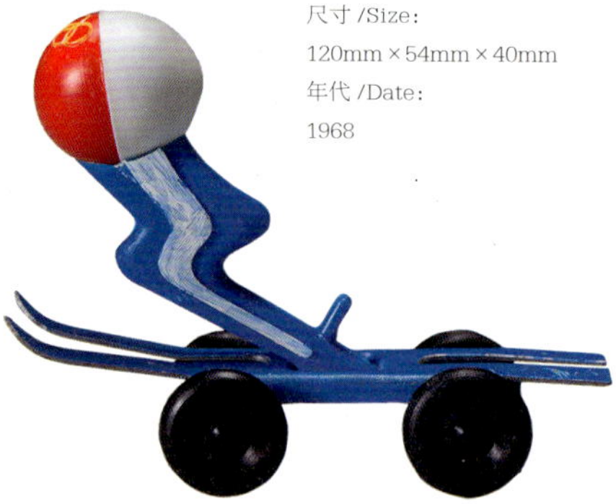

第十二届
冬季奥运会吉祥物——雪人
Mascot for the 12th
Winter Olympics – Schneemandl
尺寸 /Size：
250mm × 140mm × 210mm
年代 /Date：
1976

第十三届
冬季奥运会吉祥物——浣熊
Mascot for the 13th
Winter Olympics – Roni
尺寸 /Size：
370mm × 65mm × 270mm
年代 /Date：
1980

第十四届
冬季奥运会吉祥物——狼
Mascot for the 14th
Winter Olympics – Vucho
尺寸 /Size:
200mm × 160mm × 170mm
年代 /Date:
1984

第十五届
冬季奥运会吉祥物——北极熊
Mascots for the 15th
Winter Olympics – Howdy, Hidy
尺寸 /Size:
230mm × 133mm × 160mm
230mm × 98mm × 160mm
年代 /Date:
1988

第十六届
冬季奥运会吉祥物——冰上精灵
Mascot for the 16th
Winter Olympics – Magique
尺寸 /Size:
275mm × 80mm × 230mm
年代 /Date:
1992

第十七届
冬季奥运会吉祥物——童话中的孩子
Mascots for the 17th
Winter Olympics – Hakon, Kristin
尺寸 /Size:
240mm × 68mm × 125mm
240mm × 68mm × 125mm
年代 /Date:
1994

第十八届
冬季奥运会吉祥物——猫头鹰
Mascots for the 18th
Winter Olympics – Snowlets
尺寸 /Size:
124mm × 120mm × 140mm
年代 /Date:
1998

第十九届
冬季奥运会吉祥物——白靴兔、美洲黑熊、北美郊狼
Mascots for the 19th
Winter Olympics - Powder, Coal, Copper
尺寸 /Size:
270mm × 75mm × 190mm
390mm × 132mm × 410mm
195mm × 115mm × 181mm
年代 /Date:
2002

第二十届
冬季奥运会吉祥物——雪球、冰块
Mascots for the 20th
Winter Olympics - Neve, Gliz
尺寸 /Size:
215mm × 69mm × 130mm
215mm × 68mm × 130mm
年代 /Date:
2006

第二十一届
冬季奥运会吉祥物——海熊 、北美野人
Mascots for the 21st
Winter Olympics - Miga, Quatchi
尺寸 /Size:
320mm × 95mm × 290mm
245mm × 122mm × 180mm
年代 /Date:
2010

第二十二届
冬季奥运会吉祥物——
兔子、雪豹、北极熊
Mascots for the 22nd
Winter Olympics – Zaika,
Snow Leopard, Bely Mishka
尺寸 /Size:
300mm × 89mm × 200mm
300mm × 127mm × 245mm
250mm × 136mm × 130mm
年代 /Date:
2014

第二十三届
冬季奥会吉祥物——白老虎
Mascot for the 23rd
Winter Olympics – Soohorang
尺寸 /Size:
210mm × 120mm × 300mm
年代 /Date:
2018

第二十四届
冬季奥运会吉祥物——
熊猫冰墩墩
Mascot for the 24th
Winter Olympics –
Giant Panda Bing Dwen Dwen
尺寸 /Size:
240mm × 160mm × 250mm
年代 /Date:
2022

夏季奥运会纪念丝巾

Summer Olympic Commemorative Silk Scarf

This is the official commemorative silk scarf at each Olympics Games. Each silk scarf is composed of abstract geometric patterns, with the color of the host country. The surface is printed with obvious elements about Olympic Games, which link the Olympic and silk fabrics together.

这是每届奥运会上官方发售的纪念丝巾，每块丝巾由抽象几何图案组成，配色颇有主办国特色，表面印有明显的奥运元素，将奥运及丝织品联系在一起。

第十一届
夏季奥运会纪念丝巾
Commemorative silk scarf for the 11th Summer Olympic Games
尺寸 /Size：
1 080mm × 245mm
年代 /Date：
1936

第十四届
夏季奥运会纪念丝巾
Commemorative silk scarf for the 14th Summer Olympic Games
尺寸 /Size：
880mm × 840mm
年代 /Date：
1948

第十五届
夏季奥运会纪念丝巾
Commemorative silk scarf for the 15th Summer Olympic Games
尺寸 /Size：
740mm × 740mm
年代 /Date：
1952

第十六届
夏季奥运会纪念丝巾
Commemorative silk scarf for the 16th Summer Olympic Games
尺寸 /Size：
680mm × 670mm
年代 /Date：
1956

第十七届
夏季奥运会纪念丝巾
Commemorative silk scarf for the 17th Summer Olympic Games
尺寸 /Size：
680mm × 670mm
年代 /Date：
1960

第十八届
夏季奥运会纪念丝巾
Commemorative silk scarf for the 18th Summer Olympic Games
尺寸 /Size：
730mm × 710mm
年代 /Date：
1964

第十九届
夏季奥运会丝巾
Commemorative silk scarf for the 19th Summer Olympic Games
尺寸 /Size：
680mm × 670mm
年代 /Date：
1968

第二十届
夏季奥运会纪念丝巾
Commemorative silk scarf for the 20th Summer Olympic Games
尺寸 /Size：
660mm × 680mm
年代 /Date：
1972

第二十一届
夏季奥运会纪念丝巾
Commemorative silk scarf for the 21st Summer Olympic Games
尺寸 /Size：
680mm × 680mm
年代 /Date：
1976

第二十二届
夏季奥运会纪念丝巾
Commemorative silk scarf for the 22nd Summer Olympic Games
尺寸 /Size：
810mm × 810mm
年代 /Date：
1980

第二十三届
夏季奥运会纪念丝巾
Commemorative silk scarf for the 23rd Summer Olympic Games
尺寸 /Size:
550mm × 600mm
年代 /Date:
1984

第二十四届
夏季奥运会纪念丝巾
Commemorative silk scarf for the 24th Summer Olympic Games
尺寸 /Size:
870mm × 820mm
年代 /Date:
1988

第二十五届
夏季奥运会纪念丝巾
Commemorative silk scarf for the 25th Summer Olympic Games
尺寸 /Size:
660mm × 660mm
年代 /Date:
1992

第二十六届
夏季奥运会纪念丝巾
Commemorative silk scarf for the 26th Summer Olympic Games
尺寸 /Size：
880mm × 850mm
年代 /Date：
1996

第二十七届
夏季奥运会纪念丝巾
Commemorative silk scarf for the 27th Summer Olympic Games
尺寸 /Size：
800mm × 800mm
年代 /Date：
2000

第二十八届
夏季奥运会纪念丝巾
Commemorative silk scarf for the 28th Summer Olympic Games
尺寸 /Size：
870mm × 850mm
年代 /Date：
2004

第二十九届
夏季奥运会纪念丝巾
Commemorative silk
scarf for the 29th
Summer Olympic
Games
尺寸 /Size：
900mm × 900mm
年代 /Date：
2008

第三十届
夏季奥运会纪念丝巾
Commemorative silk
scarf for the 30th
Summer Olympic
Games
尺寸 /Size：
900mm × 900mm
年代 /Date：
2012

第三十一届
夏季奥运会纪念丝巾
Commemorative silk
scarf for the 31st
Summer Olympic
Games
尺寸 /Size：
500mm × 500mm
年代 /Date：
2016

第十八届夏季奥运会纪念章

Commemorative medal, the 18th Summer Olympics

□ 纪念章以古代奥运会图案为元素，分别铸刻有古希腊运动员传递圣火和头戴橄榄枝的运动员形象，以及第十八届奥林匹克运动会的铭文。

□ 第十八届夏季奥运会于1964年10月10—24日举行，93个国家和地区的5 140名运动员参赛，其中女子683人参加了19大项163小项。美国发射了“辛科姆”卫星，向世界各地转播奥运盛况，这在奥运会史上还是第一次。

□ With the pattern of ancient Olympic Games as an element, the two badges are respectively carved with the images of ancient Greek athletes passing the sacred flame and athletes wearing olive branches, as well as the inscriptions of the 18th Olympic Games.

□ Held from October 10 to 24, 1964, 5,140 athletes from 93 countries and regions, 683 of which were women, participated in 19 sports and 163 disciplines. The United States launched the satellite “Syncom” to transmit the real-time scenario of the court worldwide, which was the first time in the history of the Olympics.

尺寸 /Size:
Φ153mm × 10mm
数量 /Amount:
2
重量 /Weight:
417.4g
年代 /Date:
1964

第二十二届夏季奥运会牛角形酒杯

Horn-shaped wine glass, the 22nd Summer Olympics

□ 该牛角摆件为本届奥运会纪念品，同时可以作为一个酒杯来使用，但由于酒杯无法平稳放于桌上，饮酒时需一饮而尽，这也体现了斯拉夫人的热情好饮。牛角摆件做工精细，牛角质量上乘，纹路清晰，牛角两端以金属包裹作为装饰，口部金属中央嵌有本届奥运会会徽。

□ 1980 年 7 月 19 日至 8 月 3 日，第二十二届夏季奥林匹克运动会在苏联首都莫斯科举行，主会场位于莫斯科的列宁中央体育场，这是奥运会第一次来到社会主义国家。

□ The cup is the souvenir of the Olympic Games and can be used as a wine cup. However, since the wine cup cannot be placed on the table stable and the wine in it must be tossed off, the wine cup also reflects the enthusiasm of Slavonics. The pendant of the horn is exquisite with high quality and clear patterns. Both ends of the horn are decorated with metal wraps. The caliber is embedded with the emblem of the Olympic Games.

□ From July 19 to August 3, 1980, the 22nd Olympic Games was held in Moscow, the capital of Soviet Union. The main venue of the Olympic Games was Lenin Central Stadium in Moscow. This is the first time that Olympic Games has been held in a socialist country.

尺寸 /Size:
225mm × 71mm × 64mm
重量 /Weight:
151.2g
年代 /Date:
1980

尺寸 /Size:
232mm × 76mm × 60mm
重量 /Weight:
148.9g
年代 /Date:
1980

第二十三届夏季奥运会运动员彩绘镀金瓷盘

Gilded porcelain plate with colored drawing of athletes from the 23rd Summer Olympics

□ 彩瓷盘内印有四名田径运动员的图案，运动员呈运动状态：两名赛跑，一名标枪，一名铅球。瓷盘由英国百年品牌Royal Stafford制成，品牌成立于1787年，所有产品皆照英国传统方法制作而成。

□ The colored porcelain plate is printed with four athletes, which includes two racers, one javelin athlete and one shot-put athlete. The time-honored brand Royal Stafford was established in 1787 and all of its products were made in accordance with the traditional British methods.

尺寸 /Size：
Φ255mm × 30mm
年代 /Date：
1984

第二十六届夏季奥运会百年奥运高浮雕纪念瓷罐

Porcelain jar with high relief from the 26th Summer Olympics to commemorate the 100th anniversary of the Olympics

□ 瓷罐以橙色和黑色为主色调，配以红色和金色，看起来沉稳、大气。圆柱形的罐体象征着古希腊奥林匹亚建筑中的罗马柱。奥林匹亚女神高举着奥运圣火坐落于铭刻着本届奥运会会徽的黑釉锥形顶盖之上，瓷罐上雕刻有 1896 年第一届夏季奥运会海报图案，罐体绿釉与红釉交替之间的壁画图案代表着奥运会比赛项目，并且瓷罐上还镌刻着“1896—1996”“亚特兰大 1996”等字样，代表着从第一届奥运会开始，奥运会已度过了百年的光阴。高浮雕橄榄枝环绕的古希腊建筑罗马柱瓷罐手柄与罐体浑然一体。

□ The porcelain pot is mainly in orange and black, and decorated with red and gold, which looks profound and distinguished. The cylindrical pot symbolizes the marble pillar of Olympia architecture in ancient Greece. The Olympic Goddess sits on the conical black-glazed lid holding high the holy flame with the emblem of the Olympic Games. The pot is carved with the poster pattern of the first Summer Olympic Games in 1896. The mural pattern between the green glaze and the red glaze of the pot represents the competitions of Olympic Games, and the porcelain pot is engraved with the words like “1896-1996” and “Atlanta 1996”. The handle of the porcelain pot, which symbolizes that the Olympic Games have passed a hundred years since the first Olympic Games began. The marble pillar of Olympia architecture in ancient Greece is surrounded by a high-relief olive branch and it is integrated with the body part of the pot.

尺寸 /Size:
135mm × 230mm × 550mm
重量 /Weight:
4.3kg
年份 /Date:
1996

法国奥委会
奥运百年纪念大铜章

Bronze medal commemorating the 100th anniversary of the modern Olympic Games issued by the French Olympic Committee

□ The French Olympic Committee designed this commemorative bronze medal in order to commemorate the 100th anniversary of the modern Olympic Games. The bronze medal consists of two parts. The outer ring is equally divided into six parts, with six months of the year written on each side. The center is concave, and the front is written with "100-year Olympic 1896-1996" in French. A torch emits a raging flame, forming an arc along the edge of the ring. The back of the bronze medal is a woman athlete's soft body forming a perfect arc, showing the beauty of sports.

□ 为了纪念现代奥林匹克运动会举办一百周年，法国奥委会设计了这枚纪念大铜章。铜章整体分为两部分。外侧圆环被平分为六部分，两面各写了一年中的六个月份。中心圆下凹，正面用法语写着“百年奥运 1896—1996”，一把火炬喷发出熊熊燃烧的火焰，沿着圆形的边缘形成圆弧状。铜章背面是一位女运动员柔软的身体形成完美的圆弧，表现出运动之美。

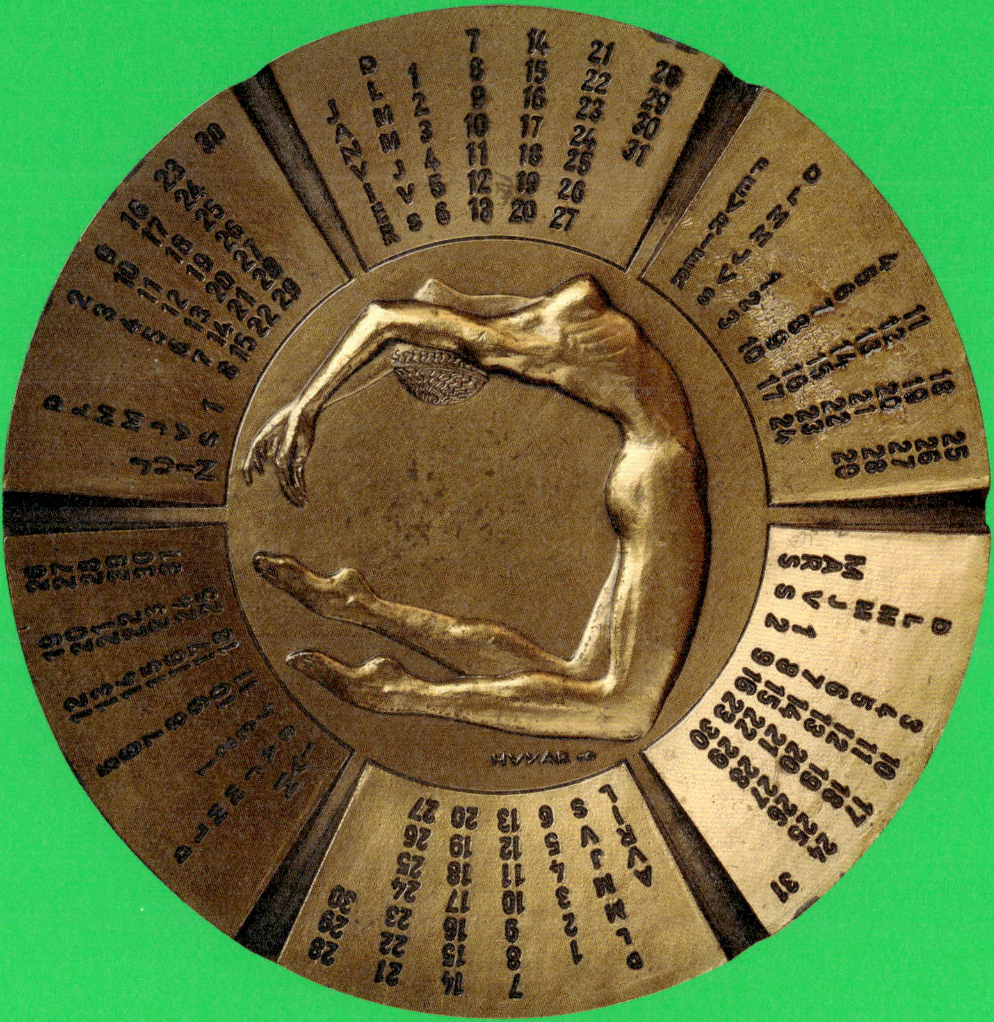

尺寸 /Size：
Φ95mm × 15mm
重量 /Weight：
617.8g
年代 /Date：
1996

奥林匹克银质勋章

Silver Olympic Order

□ In 1974, the IOC awarded the Olympic Order in three categories, namely gold, silver and bronze, in recognition of those who have made outstanding contributions in sports or achieved outstanding achievements in sports. In the middle of the medal are the five Olympic rings, and on each side is an olive branch that symbolizes peace and friendship. In 2000, Xu Yinsheng was awarded the Olympic Silver Order by the IOC.

□ 1974 年，国际奥委会为了表彰在体育工作中做出突出贡献或在体育运动中取得优异成绩者而授予奥林匹克勋章，分金质、银质、铜质三种。勋章的中间为奥林匹克的五个圆环，两边分别是一支象征和平、友谊的橄榄枝。2000 年，徐寅生被国际奥委会授予奥林匹克银质勋章。

尺寸 /Size：
400mm × 300mm
重量 /Weight：
150.9g
捐赠者 /Donated by：
徐寅生 /Xu Yinsheng
年代 /Date：
2000

徐寅生（1938—），江苏苏州人，著名男子乒乓球运动员，1959 年成为国家乒乓球集训队选手。直拍快攻打法，技术全面，战术灵活，球路变化多，素有乒坛“智多星”之称，第二十六、二十七、二十八届世界乒乓球锦标赛男团冠军主力成员，第二十八届世乒赛男双冠军。1965 年，徐寅生出任国家男队教练。1970 年任中国乒乓球队第一任总教练。在他的带领下，中国乒乓球队一举获得第三十一届世乒赛男团、女单、女双和混双 4 枚金牌，1979 年任中国乒乓球协会主席。1995 年至 1999 年任国际乒乓球联合会主席。在担任国际乒联主席期间，他为乒乓球运动进入奥运会大家庭立下了汗马功劳，并积极推动了 40 毫米大球取代 38 毫米小球。2010 年，在莫斯科举行的国际乒联代表大会上被授予国际乒联终身名誉主席称号，他也成为国际乒联历史上首位终身名誉主席。

Xu Yinsheng (1938-), a native of Suzhou, Jiangsu province, is a famous male table tennis player. In 1959, he became a player of the national table tennis training team. Straight-shooting fast attack style, comprehensive skills, flexible tactics, and many changes in the ball path. He is known as the "wisdom star" in the table tennis world, the main member of the men's team champion of the 26th, 27th and 28th World Table Tennis Championships. Men's doubles champion of the 28th World Table Tennis Championships. In 1965, Xu Yinsheng became the coach of the national men's team. Under his leadership, the Chinese table tennis team won four gold medals in the men's team, women's single, women's doubles and mixed doubles at the 31st World Table Tennis Championships. From 1995 to 1999, he served as President of the International Table Tennis Federation. During his tenure as president of the ITTF, he made great contributions to the entry of table tennis into the Olympic family, and actively promoted the replacement of 38mm small balls with 40mm balls.In 2010, at the ITTF Congress held in Moscow, he was awarded the title of Honorary Lifetime Chairman of the ITTF.

第十九届冬季奥运会高浮雕纪念瓷罐

Commemorative porcelain jar with high relief from the 19th Winter Olympics

□ 纪念瓷罐手工打造，金属罐盖被设计成方尖碑的式样，上方雕刻有本届冬奥会会徽，显示出冬奥会的神圣与庄严。瓷罐手柄以高浮雕橄榄枝衬托上方的古希腊罗马柱，凸显奥运元素。杯身两端被施以蓝釉，以简易的线条描金表现出冬奥会的运动项目，中间以四把点燃的奥运圣火分隔出四幅绘有冬奥会开幕式各国运动员高举旗帜和盐湖城风光的彩绘图案，并刻有历届冬奥会举办城市的名字。杯底呈梯形，刻有冬奥会会徽以及“Salt Lake 2002”的字样。

□ The memorial porcelain pot is hand-made. The metal lid is designed as a square-pointed stele. The emblem of the Winter Olympic Games is carved on the top of the pot, showing the sacredness and solemnity of the Winter Olympic Games. The handle of the pot highlights the Olympic elements with high-relief olive branch holding the marble pillars. The two ends of the pot are painted with blue glaze, and the simple lines depict the sports events of the Winter Olympic Games. In the middle, four burning holy flames are used to separate colored drawings depicting the athletes from different countries holding high the flags at the opening ceremony of the Winter Olympic Games and the scenery of the Salt Lake City, and the names of cities where the Olympic Winter Games were held are engraved on it. The base of the pot is trapezoidal and engraved with the emblem of the Winter Olympic Games and the words “Salt Lake 2002”.

尺寸 /Size：

160mm × 255mm × 580mm

重量 /Weight：

约 5.5kg

年代 /Date：

2002

第二十九届
夏季奥运会开幕式
道具“缶”

The “Fou Drum” used for the Opening Ceremony of the 29th Summer Olympics

□ 这是 2008 年北京奥运会开幕式表演中使用的缶，缶的造型源于 1978 年湖北随州市曾侯乙墓出土的铜鉴缶，缶四角各设有一龙形耳，腹部饰有蟠螭纹。开幕式上，2 008 个缶组成缶阵，表达 2008 年奥运会，每个缶上都写有独一无二的编号。

□ 缶，作为中国古时的一种盛器和乐器，在奥运会开幕式上使用，即有“击缶迎宾”之意，展现中华民族“有朋自远方来，不亦乐乎”的待客之道，又体现了中华文化的博大精深。表演采用了声光电高科技手段，将古代的乐队演奏进行了重新演绎，再现中国古代的礼乐文明。

□ This is the Fou used in the performance of the opening ceremony of Bejing Olympics Games. The shale of the Fou is derived from the bronze mirror Fou unearthed from the tomb of Zeng Houyi in Suizhou city, Hubei province in 1978. There is a dragon-shaped ear on each side of the Fou, and the belly is decorated with a pan-chi pattern. At the opening ceremony. 2,008 Fous formed A Fou array to express the 2008 Olympic Games, and each one has the unique number.

□ As an ancient instrument to play the prelude of the Beijing Olympics Games, the “Ji Fou Ying Bin” (welcome the guests) follows the example of ancient people. It also represents the profound Chinese culture. The performance adopts high-tech means of sound and light, reinterprets the performance of the ancient band, and reproduces the ancient Chinese ritual and music civilization.

尺寸 /Size:
1 000mm×1 000mm×850mm
重量 /Weight:
130kg
年代 /Date:
2008

第二十九届夏季奥运会火种灯摆件

Olympic Flame Lantern Ornament of the 29th Summer Olympics

□ 这是北京夏季奥运会仿火种灯制成的摆件。火种灯是保存奥林匹克圣火的工具，主要用于火种迎接、圣火点燃、圣火展示等活动。国际奥委会要求，火炬接力运行期间要保持圣火持续燃烧，以保证圣火的尊严和火炬接力的纯洁性。一旦火炬熄灭，必须用保存在火种灯里的圣火火种引燃火炬，确保奥运会开幕式上主火炬由来自奥林匹亚的圣火点燃。北京夏季奥运会火种灯的设计创意源于中国宫灯，方圆嵌套象征天圆地方，上饰祥云符号，代表祥瑞的文化含义。

□ This is an ornament made of imitation flame lantern for the Beijing Summer Olympics. The flame lantern is a tool for preserving the Olympic Holy Flame, which is mainly used for activities like welcoming, igniting and displaying the holy flame. The IOC requires that the holy flame should keep burning during the torch relay to ensure the dignity of the holy flame and the purity of the torch relay. Once the torch is extinguished, it must be ignited with the flame stored in the flame lantern to ensure that the main torch at the opening ceremony of Olympic Games is ignited by the holy flame from the Olympia. The design idea of the flame lantern for the Beijing Olympic Games originates from the Chinese palace lanterns. The square-circle nest symbolizes the round sky and square ground, and the symbol of Xiangyun(clouds) on it represents “good luck”.

尺寸 /Size：
258mm × 125mm × 365mm
重量 /Weight：
3 310.1g
年代 /Date：
2008

第二十九届夏季奥运会国际技术官员服

Suit of International Technical Official at the 29th Summer Olympics

□ 该套服装为第二十九届北京奥运会国际技术官员服，官员服款式为西装样式，其颜色为蓝色，左胸上为电脑绣花而成的奥运会会徽中国印。

□ 2008 年北京夏季奥运会共创造 43 项新世界纪录及 132 项新奥运纪录，共有 87 个国家和地区在赛事中取得奖牌，中国以 51 枚金牌居金牌榜榜首，是奥运历史上首个登上金牌榜首的亚洲国家。本届奥运会上的技术官员由国际单项体育联合会确定，通常包括裁判员以及其他体育官员。国内技术官员为辅助裁判，国际技术官员为执法裁判。

□ This is the uniform of the international technical official in the 29th Beijing Olympic Games. It is in blue and a suit style on the left chest of which is printed with the Olympic emblem by computer embroidery.

□ 43 new world records and 132 new Olympic records were born in the 2008 Beijing Olympic Games with 87 countries and regions won medals in the competitions. China, with 51 gold medals altogether, ranked the first in the gold medal tally in the Games and became the first Asian country topping the gold medal tally. Technical offers in the 2008 Beijing Olympic Games, including referees and other sports officers, are determined by the General Association of International Sports Federations. Domestic technical officers served as assistant referees, and international officers as the referees of enforcement.

尺寸 /Size:
186/96A
捐赠者 /Donated by:
郭蓓 /Guo Bei
年代 /Date:
2008

国际乒联名人堂荣誉牌

ITTF Hall of Fame Honor Plate

□ 这是王励勤 2005 年入选国际乒联名人堂时获得的荣誉牌。国际乒联名人堂创设于 1993 年，只有在世乒赛或奥运会上获得五枚以上金牌的运动员才有资格列为候选。

□ 王励勤（1978—），上海人，1993 年入选国家队。2001 年大阪第四十六届世乒赛，王励勤获得男单、男双、男团项目的三个冠军。2004 年，王励勤重获世乒赛的男团项目冠军，并于雅典奥运会击败瓦尔德内尔获得冠军。2007 年在第四十九届世乒赛上，夺得男单冠军。2008 年北京奥运会，王励勤获男子团体金牌和单打铜牌。

□ This is the honorary medal that Wang Liqin received when he was inducted into the ITTF Hall of Fame which was created in 1993, and only athletes who have won five or more gold medals at the World Table Tennis Championships or the Olympics are eligible to be listed as candidates.

□ Wang Liqin (1978-), born in Shanghai, was selected as a member of the national team in 1993. In 2001, Wang Liqin won the three championships of the men's singles, men's doubles and men's team at the 46th World Table Tennis Championships in Osaka. In 2004, Wang Liqin re-won the championship of the men's team in the World Table Tennis Championships and defeated Waldner in the Athens Olympic Games. In 2007, he won the championship of the men's singles at the 49th World Table Tennis Championships. In the 2008 Beijing Olympics, Wang Liqin won the men's team gold medal and men's single bronze medal.

尺寸 /Size:

262mm × 332mm × 18mm

重量 /Weight:

1 326.9g

借展者 /Borrower of Exhibition:

王励勤 /Wang Liqin

年代 /Date:

2005

第二十九届夏季奥运会赛用泳衣

Swimsuit worn by Wu Minxia at the 29th Summer Olympics

□ 泳衣为北京夏季奥运会上吴敏霞比赛夺得冠军时所穿，蓝紫色渐变款，连身设计，胸口印有中国国旗。

□ 吴敏霞（1985—），上海人，中国历史上首位女性奥运“五金”冠军。1998 年入选中国国家队。曾获得雅典奥运会女子双人 3 米板冠军、北京奥运会女子双人 3 米板冠军、里约热内卢奥运会女子跳水双人 3 米板冠军、伦敦奥运会女子跳水双人 3 米板冠军和单人 3 米板冠军，并获得中国十佳劳伦斯冠军奖最佳女运动员奖和上海市体育事业白玉兰终身杰出成就奖。

□ The one-piece swimsuit of Wu Minxia when she won the competition at the Summer Olympics in Beijing features a gradient color of blue and purple with the national flag of China printed on the chest.

□ Wu Minxia (1985-), born in Shanghai, the first female five-time Olympic gold medalist. Wu was elected to the national team in 1998. She ever won gold medals in the Synchronized Diving 3-meter Springboard Women in 2004 Athens Olympic Games, Synchronized Diving 3-meter Springboard Women in 2008 Beijing Olympic Games, Synchronized Diving 3-meter Springboard Women in 2016 Rio de Janeiro Olympic Games, Synchronized Diving 3-meter Springboard Women and 3-meter Springboard Women in 2012 London Olympic Games. She was also awarded the Best Female Athlete in China Top Ten Benefiting Laureus Sport For Good and the Life Achievement Award of Magnolia Awards of Shanghai Sports.

尺寸 /Size：
290mm × 640mm
捐赠者 /Donated by：
吴敏霞 /Wu Minxia
年代 /Date：
2008

第二十八届 夏季奥运会 男子 110 米栏 赛用运动鞋

Sneakers worn by Liu Xiang in the men's 110m hurdles at the 28th Summer Olympics

□ 这是刘翔参加雅典夏季奥运会男子110 米栏夺冠时所穿的运动鞋。鞋子以红、白两色为主色调，脚背处有拉链和搭扣设计，前方写有刘翔的签名，鞋底有合金钉，用于防滑。

□ 刘翔（1983—），上海人，中国男子田径队 110 米栏运动员。中国体育田径史上、也是亚洲田径史上第一个集奥运会、室内室外世锦赛、国际田联大奖赛总决赛冠军和世界纪录保持者多项荣誉于一身的运动员。2004 年雅典奥运会上，刘翔以 12 秒 91 的成绩追平了英国选手科林杰克逊保持的男子 110 米栏世界纪录夺冠。2006 年瑞士洛桑田径超级大奖赛上，以 12 秒 88 的成绩打破了保持 13 年的男子 110 米栏世界纪录夺冠。

□ These are sneakers worn by Liu Xiang when he won the men's 110-meter hurdles at the Athens Summer Olympics. The sneakers are mainly red and white, with zippers and buckles on the instep. Liu Xiang's signature in front, the sole has alloy studs for slip resistance.

□ Liu Xiang (1983-), born in Shanghai, a 110-meter hurdles athlete of the Chinese men's athletics team. He is also the first athlete in the history of Chinese athletics sports and Asian athletics to gather many honors from the Olympic Games, the indoor and outdoor world championships, the champion of IAAF World Grand Prix Finals and the world record holder. At the 2004 Athens Olympic Games, Liu Xiang equalled the 110-meter hurdles world record held by British player Colin Jackson with the score of 12.91 seconds. At the 2006 Super Grand Prix in Lausanne, Switzerland, Liu Xiang broke the 110-meter hurdles world record kept for 13 years long with the score of 12.88 seconds.

尺寸 /Size：

43 码

借展者 /Borrower of Exhibition：

上海市青少年发展基金会

/Shanghai Youth Development Foundation

年代 /Date：

2004

第二十九届夏季奥运会赛用鲨鱼皮泳衣

Sharkskin swimsuit worn by Liu Zige at the 29th Summer Olympics

□ 鲨鱼皮泳衣为模仿鲨鱼的皮肤制成的泳衣，可减少泳衣表面与水的摩擦力，被广泛应用于游泳比赛中，于 2010 年 5 月被禁用。泳衣连体设计，总体呈黑色，右胸口上方有使用者刘子歌的签名。

□ 刘子歌（1989—），辽宁本溪人。2007 年进入国家队，2008 年刘子歌在北京奥运会女子 200 米蝶泳决赛中以打破世界纪录的成绩获得金牌。2010 年，刘子歌获得 2009 年 CCTV 体坛风云人物最佳女运动员奖。

□ The shark-skin like swimsuit imitates the skin of shark to reduce the friction between swimsuit and water. It was commonly used in swimming competitions before May 2010 until it was banned. Featuring one-piece design, the swimsuit is simple in black, above the right chest is the signature of the user Liu Zige.

□ Liu Zige (1989-), born in Benxi City, Liaoning province. Liu Zige was elected to the national team in 2007. She won the gold medal in 200-meter Butterfly Women in 2008 Beijing Olympic Games with a result that broke the world record.In 2010, Liu was awarded the Best Female Athlete, 2009 CCTV Sports Personality of the Year.

尺寸 /Size:
270mm × 1280mm
捐赠者 /Donated by:
刘子歌 /Liu Zige
年代 /Date:
2008

第二十九届 夏季奥运会 赛用拳套

Gloves worn by Zou Shiming at the 29th Summer Olympics

第二展厅

EXHIBITION HALL II

□ 该拳击手套为邹市明夺冠时使用，以蓝色为底，在顶部的白色部分有邹市明签名。

□ 邹市明（1981—），贵州遵义人，中国著名拳击运动员。2008 年 8 月 16 日，第 29 届北京夏季奥运会男子轻量级（48 公斤级）1/8 决赛，中国选手邹市明和法国选手乌巴利点数 3 比 3 战平，最终裁判认定邹市明获胜，他惊险地晋级八强。数日后，邹市明在决赛中轻松战胜蒙古选手塞尔丹巴，夺得中国拳击历史上第一枚奥运会金牌。2012 年，伦敦奥运会男子拳击轻量级（49 公斤级）决赛中，邹市明最终以 13 比 10 战胜泰国名将彭布莱恩卫冕拳坛冠军。

□ The boxing gloves were worn by Zou Shiming when he won the first prize, it is of the blue base, and the white part on the top was signed by Zou Shiming.

□ Zou Shiming (1981-), born in Zunyi, Guizhou province, a famous Chinese boxing athlete. On August 16, 2008, in the 1/8 final of the Men's Fly Weight (48kg) of the 29th Beijing Olympic Games, Chinese competitor Zou Shiming and French competitor N.Oubaali drew 3-3, the referee judged that Zou Shiming won thus ranking the 8th. After several days, Zou Shiming easily won the first gold medal in Chinese boxing history by winning Mongolian competitor Serdanba in the final. In 2012, during the men's boxing lightweight (49 kg) finals of the London Olympics, Zou Shiming finally won the famous Thai athlete Pen Bryan, becoming the defending champion at a score of 13 to 10.

尺寸 /Size：
380mm × 180mm
重量 /Weight：
10 盎司 /oz
捐赠者 /Donated by：
邹市明 /Zou Shiming
年代 /Date：
2008

英国帆船冠军赛激光雷迪尔级优胜奖杯

British Sailing Laser Radial Championship trophy (Xu Lijia)

□ 这是徐莉佳获得的英国帆船冠军赛激光雷迪尔级优胜奖杯。奖杯以三角和曲线组合成帆船的样式，杯座上刻有比赛名称、地点及获奖项目：韦茅斯－波特兰国立帆船学院，帆船冠军赛激光雷迪尔级优胜奖杯。

□ 徐莉佳（1987—），上海人。2006 年 8 月 6 日，在美国加州举行的世界帆船帆板锦标赛上，徐莉佳以总成绩 42 分，提前一轮的绝对优势，夺得激光级女子组冠军，这是中国帆船项目开展 26 年以来，首次在帆船帆板项目上夺得奥运项目世界冠军。2012 年 8 月 6 日，伦敦奥运会帆船激光雷迪尔级女子单人艇的比赛中，徐莉佳一路领先夺得冠军。这是中国乃至亚洲帆船史上的首枚奥运金牌。8 月 19 日，徐莉佳成为了伦敦奥运会闭幕式中国代表团的旗手。2012 年 11 月，获国际帆联最佳女运动员奖。

□ The trophy awarded to Xu Lijia at British Sailing Laser Radial Championships. It is shaped like a sailing vessel with a triangle and curves. The base is engraved with the name, place and winning sport of the competition, namely Weymouth and Portland National Sailing Academy, Trophy of Laser Radial World Championship.

□ Xu Lijia (1987-) was born in Shanghai. On August 6, 2006, at the World Windsurfing Championships held in California, Xu Lijia won the world championship of women's laser radial with a total score of 42 points. This is the first time for Chinese sailing athletes to win the world championship in windsurfing in Olympics over the 26 years. On August 6, 2012, Xu Lijia won the championship of women's laser radial single in the London 2012 Olympics. This is the first Olympic gold medal in the history of the sailing event in China and even Asia. On August 19, Xu Lijia served as the flag-bearer of the Chinese delegation at the closing ceremony of the London 2012 Olympics. In November 2012, she was awarded as the Best Woman Athlete by the World Sailing.

尺寸 /Size：
270mm × 150mm × 570mm
重量 /Weight：
2 312.7g
捐赠者 /Donated by：
徐莉佳 /Xu Lijia
年代 /Date：
2008

第三十一届夏季奥运会赛用同款自行车头盔

Bicycle helmet as same as the one used by Zhong Tianshi at the 31st Summer Olympics

□ 头盔使用了国粹京剧之中的“脸谱”作为主题，以花木兰脸谱为主要元素，头盔的侧面饰有中国传统祥云符号，并装点有国旗元素；头盔的后侧点缀的是牡丹花瓣，寓意着这次中国队的奥运之行像花朵那样开得灿烂。头盔后方是采用纯黑色毛笔字写下的“钟”字，表明这是钟天使专属头盔。

□ 2016 年第三十一届里约热内卢夏季奥运赛场上，自行车运动员钟天使和宫金杰两人相继刷新奥运会和世界纪录，为中国赢得自行车项目的奥运首金，两位姑娘佩戴的头盔更是让现场刮起了另类的红色旋风。“万里赴戎机，关山度若飞”，小将钟天使正如花木兰一般，在场上不惧任何对手的挑战，充分展现了中国女性的巾帼风采。此外，在 2020 年东京奥运会上，钟天使更是携队友鲍珊菊再为我国夺得一枚场地自行车女子团体竞速赛金牌。

□ The helmet takes the “facial mask” in Peking Opera as the theme and the facial mask of Hua Mulan (a Chinese heroin in legend) as the major element, decorated with Chinese auspicious cloud patterns and national flag on the sides. On the back of the helmet there are pony petals, meaning the blooming of Chinese teams as flowers in the Olympic trip. The character “Zhong” written by brush in black indicates the exclusiveness of helmet.

□ In the 31st Rio de Janeiro Summer Olympic Games in 2016, Chinese cyclists Zhong Tianshi and Gong Jinjie set a new Olympic and world record, winning the first gold medal in cycling track for China. Helmets that the two girls wore ever brought the spot a special red whirlwind. “For miles and miles, the army march along and cross the mountain barriers as in flight”. As tough as Hua Mulan, Zhong Tianshi behaved fearlessly indefatigable in the competition and fully represented the architype of Chinese women. In addition, at the 2020 Tokyo Olympics, Zhong Tianshi and her teammate Bao Shanju won another gold medal for our country in the women’s team sprint race on cycling venues.

尺寸 /Size：
头围 56~58cm 小码
捐赠者 /Donated by：
张栋良 /Zhang Dongliang
年代 /Date：
2016

第三十一届
夏季奥运会
赛用乒乓球拍和球

Table Tennis Racket and Ball used by Xu Xin at the 31st Summer Olympics

□ 这是许昕在第三十一届里约热内卢夏季奥运会乒乓球男团比赛上使用的乒乓球拍和球，上面皆有许昕的签名。

□ 许昕（1990—），江苏徐州人，2001年进入上海曹燕华乒乓培训学校学习，2003年进入上海市乒乓球队，2006年入选国家二队。2013年乒乓球世界杯赛中，许昕获得男单冠军，成为中国首位获得男单世界冠军的左手运动员。2016年里约热内卢夏季奥运会乒乓球男团决赛中，许昕与马龙、张继科以3比1击败日本队，获得冠军，实现奥运男团三连冠。许昕是中国乒乓球历史上首位在世界三大赛中赢得男单冠军的左手直板球员。凭借着过硬的专业技术，2016年12月，许昕正式选入国际乒联名人堂，在国际上为自己争得了一席之地。2020年东京夏季奥运会上，许昕再次夺得乒乓球男团冠军，中国乒乓球队实现奥运男团四连冠。

□ These are the table tennis racket and ball used by Xu Xin in the men's table tennis competition at the 31st Rio de Janeiro Summer Olympics, with Xu Xin's signature on them.

□ Xu Xin (1990-), born in Xuzhou, Jiangsu province, entered Shanghai Cao Yanhua Table Tennis Training School in 2001, entered Shanghai Table Tennis Team in 2003, and was selected as the member of No. 2 National Team in 2006. In the Table Tennis World Cup in 2013, Xu Xin won the championship of men's singles and became the first left-hand player in China to win the championship of men's singles. In the finals of the men's team of the 2016 Rio Summer Olympics, Xu Xin, Ma Long and Zhang Jike defeated the Japanese team with 3-1, winning the championship and realizing the third consecutive title of the men's team in the Olympic Games. Xu Xin is the first left-hand pen-hold grip player in the history of Chinese table tennis that won the championship of the men's singles in the World Three Competitions. With excellent professional skills, Xu Xin officially elected to the International Table Tennis Hall in December 2016, winning a place for himself internationally. At the 2020 Tokyo Summer Olympics Xu Xin and his teammates won the table tennis men's team championship again, and the Chinese table tennis team achieved four consecutive Olympic men's team championships.

尺寸 /Size:
乒乓球拍 /Table tennis bat:
155mm × 263mm × 15mm
乒乓球 /Table tennis ball:
Φ40mm
捐赠者 /Donated by:
许昕 /Xu Xin
年代 /Date:
2016

国际奥委会
“运动普及”纪念章
International Olympic Committee (IOC) “SPORT FOR ALL” Souvenir Medal

□ The medal is rectangular in shape and silver throughout, the words “SPORT FOR ALL” are written on the front in English and French. The International Olympic Committee issues medals to promote universal sport.

□ 纪念章呈长方形，通体银色，正面使用英法两种文字写有“运动普及”字样。国际奥委会发行纪念章用于推广普及体育运动。

尺寸 /Size：
70mm × 110mm × 4mm
重量 /Weight：
200g
年代 /Date：
当代 /Contemporary

第三展厅
EXHIBITION HALL III

活力之城

A CITY FULL OF VITALITY

第三展厅

EXHIBITION HALL III

精彩纷呈·赛事之都
A CAPITAL OF EXCITING EVENTS
一百多年前，第二届远东运动会在上海举行，这是中国第一次举办国际性体育大赛，《申报》记载"开前所未有之奇观"。以此历数，三届远东运动会、两届民国全运会，两届新中国全运会，首届东亚运动会，乃至世乒赛、女足世界杯等众多国际顶级赛事连缀于上海的百年历史演进之中。赛事之都，由来已久。
More than a hundred years ago, the 2nd Olympic Far Eastern Championship Games (also known as the Far Eastern Championships, Far Eastern Games or Far East Games) was held in Shanghai. That was the first time China held an international sports competition, and Shun Pao recorded the Games as "an unprecedented spectacle." So far, in the century-old history of Shanghai, three Far Eastern Championship Games, two National Games of the Republic of China, two National Games of the People's Republic of China, the first East Asian Games, the World Table Tennis Championships, the FIFA Women's World Cup and many other top international events have been held here in the city. With the historic legacy of hosting some of the world's top sports games, Shanghai has a long history as the capital of events.
成果荟萃 体育盛会
Fruitful Results of Hosting Sports Events
改革开放以后，上海举办了第五届、第八届全国运动会等综合性运动会，有力地促进了上海体育的快速发展。运动会的举办为上海这座社会主义国际化大都市在世界面前树立了新的开放形象，成为上海不可或缺的城市名片。
After the reform and opening-up, Shanghai hosted the 5th and 8th National Games and other comprehensive sports games, which effectively promoted the rapid development of sports in Shanghai. The hosting of the events has established Shanghai, a socialist international metropolis, as a new, open and inclusive city in front of the world, and has become indispensable to the glamor of Shanghai.
第五届全国运动会
第五届全国运动会于1983年9月18日至10月1日在上海举行。这届运动会是中国改革开放以后的一次体育盛会，也是首次在首都以外的城市举办的全国运动会，上海代表团获得33枚金牌、35枚银牌、30枚铜牌，奖牌总数列全国第一，金牌数名列全国第二。
The 5th National Games
The 5th National Games of the People's Republic of China were held in Shanghai from September 18 to October 1, 1983. The sports event was held after China's reform and opening-up, and it is the first National Games held in a city outside the capital Beijing. Shanghai won 33 golds, 35 silvers, and 30 bronzes, ranking first in the total number of medals and second in the number of gold medals.
精彩纷呈·赛事之都
2015年世界花样滑冰锦标赛
精彩纷呈·赛事之都
品牌赛事 城市名片
世界高尔夫球锦标赛·汇丰冠军赛

国际赛车场
PRIX
Heineken
友好桥梁·城

上海市运动会奖牌

Medal of Shanghai Municipal Games

□ 1952 年 6 月 10 日，毛泽东同志发表了“发展体育运动，增强人民体质”的题词，为我国体育发展奠定了重要的思想基础，上海的群众性基层体育竞赛迅速开展。1953 年 5 月 30 日，上海市第一届运动会（又称首届人民体育大会）在虹口体育场开幕。迄今，上海市已举办了 16 届市运动会。从第五届开始，每隔 4 年举办 1 次，上海市运动会已成为检阅各个历史时期全市体育运动水平的传统体育盛会。21 世纪以来，上海市运动会以奥运、全运项目为布局原则，落实奥运争光计划和全民健身国家战略，突出竞技体育后备人才培养和选拔，服务于“全球著名体育城市”和“健康上海”建设。

□ On June 10, 1952, Chairman Mao Zedong proposed the slogan of “development of the sport to enhance the people’s physique”, laying an important ideological foundation for China’s sports career, and the mass grass-roots sports competition in Shanghai was carried out rapidly.
On May 30, 1953, the 1st Shanghai Municipal Games, also known as the 1st People’s Sports Conference, opened in Hongkou Stadium. By far, Shanghai has successfully held 16 municipal sports games. But after the 5th session, it has been held every four years, which has become a traditional sports event to evaluate the sports competence across the whole city in different historical periods. Since the new century, Shanghai Municipal Games has taken the sports of Olympics and National Games as the planning principle, implemented the plan of competing for honors in the Olympic Games and the national strategy of sport for all, which highlighted the training and selection of reserve talent for competitive sports and served the construction of “a world-famous sports city” and “healthy Shanghai.”

上海市第一届运动会
（即上海市人民体育大会）
第一名奖牌
Medal for the first place at
the 1st Shanghai Municipal
Games
(namely Shanghai People's
Sports Conference)
尺寸 /Size：
Φ35mm × 1mm
重量 /Weight：
15.6g
年代 /Date：
1953

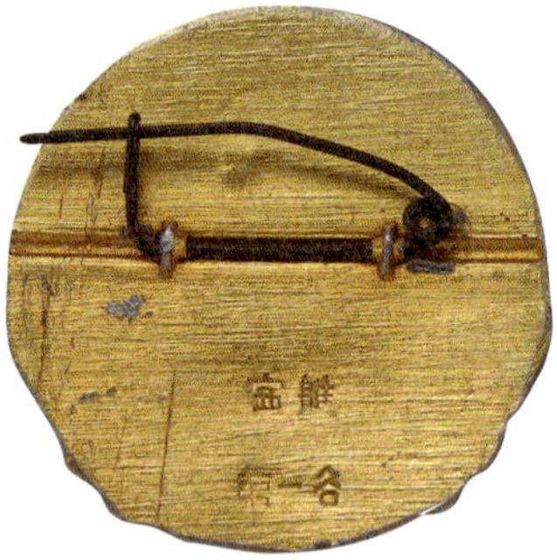

上海市第二届运动会
赛艇第一名奖牌
Medal for the first place in rowing at the 2nd Shanghai Municipal Games
尺寸 /Size：
Φ30mm × 1mm
重量 /Weight：
14.2g
年代 /Date：
1959

上海市第四届运动会
第一名奖牌
Medal for the first place at the 4th Shanghai Municipal Games
尺寸 /Size：
30mm × 28mm × 1mm
重量 /Weight：
3g
年代 /Date：
1964

上海市第五届运动会
名次章
Ranking medal from
the 5th Shanghai
Municipal Games
尺寸 /Size:
28mm × 34mm × 1mm
带链长 57mm
重量 /Weight:
7.7g
年代 /Date:
1974

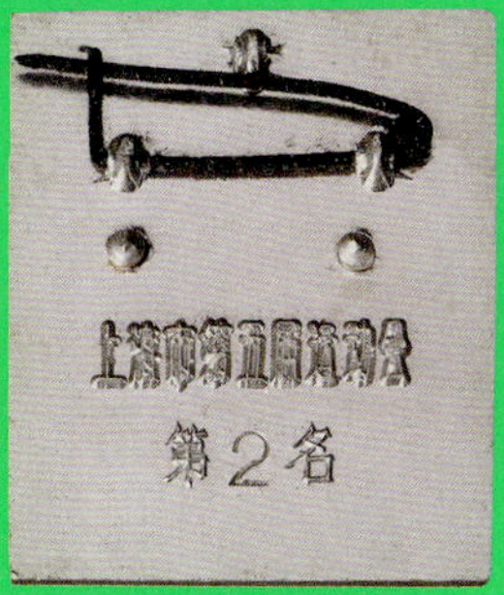

上海市第五届运动会
男子 100 米蛙泳
第二名奖章
Medal for the second
place in men's 100m
breaststroke at the 5th
Shanghai Municipal
Games
尺寸 /Size:
30mm × 35mm × 1mm
重量 /Weight:
6.6g
年代 /Date:
1974

上海市第五届运动会
会徽纪念章
Commemorative badge
of the 5th Shanghai
Municipal Games
尺寸 /Size:
Φ21mm × 1mm
重量 /Weight:
1.7g
年代 /Date:
1974

上海市第六届运动会
名次章
Ranking medal from
the 6th Shanghai
Municipal Games
尺寸 /Size：
23mm × 35mm × 1mm
重量 /Weight：
3.7g
年代 /Date：
1978

上海市第七届运动会
名次章
Ranking medals from
the 7th Shanghai
Municipal Games
尺寸 /Size：
37mm × 45mm × 1mm
重量 /Weight：
7.3g
年代 /Date：
1982

上海市第八届运动会
名次章
Ranking medals from
the 8th Shanghai
Municipal Games
尺寸 /Size：
50mm × 51mm × 1mm
带链长 70mm
重量 /Weight：
15.9g
年代 /Date：
1986

上海市第九届运动会
第二名奖章
Medal for the second
place at the 9th
Shanghai Municipal
Games
尺寸 /Size：
Φ55mm × 1mm
重量 /Weight：
14.9g
年代 /Date：
1990

乒乓球运动员用球拍

Table Tennis Racket used by Table Tennis Players

李富荣用球拍

Table Tennis Racket used by Li Furong

□ 这是李富荣使用的乒乓球拍。

□ 李富荣（1942— ），上海人，1957年进行乒乓球训练；1958年进入上海乒乓球队，同年被选入国家乒乓球集训队。1961年李富荣获得第二十六届世界乒乓球锦标赛男子单打亚军，之后与队友合作，又夺得第26、27、28、31届世界乒乓球锦标赛男子团体冠军。1974—1981年，执教中国乒乓球男队，1981年的第三十六届世界乒乓球锦标赛，李富荣率队实现全部七项冠军的大包揽。1984年李富荣被评为中华人民共和国成立35年来杰出教练员之一；2015年5月3日，中国乒乓球协会向李富荣颁发"中国乒乓球运动终身成就奖"，表彰李富荣对中国乒乓球运动的发展作出的杰出贡献。

□ This is the table tennis racket used by Li Furong.

□ Li Furong (1942-), born in Shanghai, conducted table tennis training in 1957; entered the Shanghai Table Tennis Team in 1958, and was selected as the National Table Tennis Team in the same year. In 1961, Li Furong won the second prize of the men's singles in the 26th World Table Tennis Championships, and then worked with teammates to win the first prize of the men's team in the 26th, 27th, 28th and 31st World Table Tennis Championships. From 1974 to 1981, Li Furong served as the coach of Chinese men's team, and in the 36th World Table Tennis Championships in 1981, the team led by him got the slam definition. In 1984, Li Furong was awarded as one of the outstanding coaches in the thirty-five years since the founding of the People's Republic of China; on May 3, 2015, the China Table Tennis Association awarded Li Furong the "China Table Tennis Lifetime Achievement Award" to commend Li Furong for his outstanding contribution to the development of table tennis in China.

尺寸 /Size：

145mm × 225mm × 10mm

捐赠者 /Donated by：

李富荣 /Li Furong

年代 /Date：

当代 /Contemporary

郑敏之签名球拍

Table Tennis Racket used by Zheng Minzhi

□ 这是郑敏之使用的乒乓球拍，上有郑敏之签名。

□ 郑敏之（1945—），生于上海，祖籍广东中山。1958年入选上海市乒乓球队，1960年入选国家乒乓球集训队。1961年在全国比赛中战胜了世界冠军邱钟惠，开始了向世界巅峰攀登。郑敏之是横板球手，擅长削球，防守稳健。1963年第一次代表国家参加第二十七届世界乒乓球锦标赛，就与张燮林合作打败了当时的世界混双冠军——日本选手荻村伊智朗和松崎君代。1965年，她与林慧卿一起，战胜了日本队，中国女队首次捧得考比伦杯；同年，参加第二十八届世界乒乓球锦标赛，与林慧卿、李赫男组成的女子团体获冠军，与林慧卿合作的女子双打也获冠军。1974年后，郑敏之先后被聘任为国家乒乓球队教练、副领队兼副总教练。1979年出任国家乒乓球协会副主席，1987年，被委任为国家体委训练竞赛二司副司长。郑敏之先后四次获得国家体育运动荣誉勋章，并曾任中国人民政治协商会会议第五届委员、第六届全国政协常委。

□ This is the table tennis racket used by Zheng Minzhi, with her signature on it.

□ Zheng Minzhi(1945-), born in Shanghai, ancestral home is Zhongshan, Guangdong province. She was selected as Shanghai Table Tennis Team in 1958 and the National Table Tennis Team in 1960. In 1961, she beat Qiu Zhonghui who was the world champion in a nationwide competition and began to climb to the top of the world. Zheng Minzhi is a handshake grip player who is good at chopping and has a steady defense. In 1963, she participated in the 27th World Table Tennis Championship for the first time on behalf of the state, and cooperated with Zhang Xielin to defeat the then world champion of mixed doubles, the Japanese athletes Ogimura Ichiro and Matsuzaki Kimiyo. In 1965, she won the Japanese team together with Lin Huiqing, and the Chinese women's table tennis team won the M Corbillon Cup for the first time; in the same year, she participated in the 28th World Table Tennis Championship, and the women's team composed of Lin Huiqing and Li Henan won the championship, and the women's doubles played with Lin Huiqing won the championship, too. After 1974, Zheng Minzhi was successively appointed as the coach, deputy leader and deputy chief coach of the National Table Tennis Team. She served as Vice President of the National Table Tennis Association in 1979 and was appointed Deputy Director of the Second Training and Competition Department of General Administration of Sport of China in 1987. Zheng Minzhi was awarded the Honorary Medal of National Sports four times, and once served as the fifth member of the Chinese People's Political Consultative Conference and the sixth Standing Committee of the National Political Consultative Conference.

尺寸 /Size：
155mm × 265mm × 10mm
捐赠者 /Donated by：
郑敏之 /Zheng Minzhi
年代 /Date：
当代 /Contemporary

曹燕华签名球拍

Table Tennis Racket used by Cao Yanhua

□ 这是曹燕华使用的乒乓球拍，上有曹燕华签名。

□ 曹燕华(1962—)，上海人，1977年进入国家队。在曹燕华职业生涯中共荣获国内外各项比赛冠军56项，其中世界冠军7项，她是中国女子乒乓球队员中获世界冠军最多的选手。是我国目前唯一获7个世界冠军的女运动员，为中国乒乓球事业做出了突出贡献。曹燕华的技术打法是直板弧圈球结合快攻。她开创了女子直板全台单面拉的全新打法，正手弧圈旋转强、前冲。现为上海市人大代表、上海曹燕华乒乓培训学校校长的她，一直致力于乒乓球后备人才的培养和体育文化的传承与弘扬，使上海乒乓球运动项目薪火相传。

□ This is the table tennis racket used by Cao Yanhua, with her signature on it.

□ Cao Yanhua (1962-), born in Shanghai, entered the national team in 1977. In Cao Yanhua's career, she won 56 championships at home and abroad, including 7 world championships. She won the most world championship among Chinese women's table tennis players. She is the only female athlete who has won seven world champions in China at present, making outstanding contributions to China's table tennis industry. Cao Yanhua used pen-grip two-side loop tactics with the combination of smash. She created a new style of play of backhand block with forehand of women's pen-hold grip in full court, fast and accelerated loop and spin of forehand. She is now the representative of Shanghai Municipal People's Congress and the president of Shanghai Cao Yanhua Table Tennis Training School. She has been committed to the cultivation of reserve talents for table tennis and the inheritance and promotion of sports culture, so that the Shanghai Table Tennis Sports Project has been spread.

尺寸 /Size:
150mm × 233mm × 15mm
捐赠者 /Donated by:
曹燕华 /Cao Yanhua
年代 /Date:
当代 /Contemporary

中国象棋冠军赛奖杯

Trophy of the Chinese Chess Championship

□ 这是胡荣华获得的中国象棋冠军赛奖杯。中国象棋冠军赛奖杯又称五羊奖杯，奖杯掐丝珐琅工艺制作，杯身主要为蓝色珐琅釉，装点以中国传统纹饰。杯脚和杯耳为金色，由铜制作而成。奖杯上刻有“胡荣华 中国象棋冠军赛 五羊杯”字样以及主办单位，另外还有前四届比赛的时间和冠军。

□ “五羊杯”中国象棋冠军赛是中国象棋最高水平的赛事之一，由《羊城晚报》和《新体育》杂志社发起，1981 年举办首届。1985 年起，全国政协副主席霍英东开始赞助“五羊杯”。1985 年 1 月 10—14 日，第五届“五羊杯”中国象棋冠军赛在广州市文化公园举行。参加比赛的有河北李来群、上海胡荣华、湖北柳大华和广东吕钦，胡荣华获得冠军。

□ This is the trophy of the Chinese Chess Championship by Hu Ronghua. The Chinese Chess Championship Trophy is also known as the “Five-Ram Trophy”. The trophy was made in silk-wound enamel technique. The body of the trophy is mainly glazed with blue enamel and decorated with traditional Chinese patterns. The feet and ears of the trophy are gold, made of copper. The trophy is engraved with the words “Hu Ronghua Chinese Chess Championship, Five-Ram Trophy” and the organizer, as well as the time and champion of the first four sessions.

□ The “Five-Ram Cup” Chinese Chess Championship is one of the highest levels of chess competitions in China, which was launched by *Yangcheng Evening News* and *New Physical Education*. The first session was held in 1981. Since 1985, Huo Yingdong, Vice Chairman of the National Committee of the Chinese People's Political and Consultative Conference, sponsored the “Five-Ram Cup” Championship. From January 10 to 14, 1985, the 5th “Five-Ram Cup” Chinese Chess Championship was held in Guangzhou Cultural Park. The participants included Li Laiqun (from Hebei province), Hu Ronghua (from Shanghai), Liu Dahua (from Hubei province) and Lyu Qin (from Guangdong province), and Hu Ronghua won the champion.

尺寸 /Size:
210mm × 120mm × 372mm
重量 /Weight:
938.8g
捐赠者 /Donated by:
胡荣华 /Hu Ronghua
年代 /Date:
1985

胡荣华（1945—），上海人，中国象棋界一代宗师，当代象棋学派的主要奠基人，20 世纪最杰出的象棋手之一，棋界人称“胡司令”。胡荣华 15 岁时首次参加全国赛即夺得冠军，跻身于全国一流棋手之列。他曾夺得 14 次全国象棋个人赛冠军，其中 1960 年至 1979 年创造了十连冠的奇迹。1982 年国家体委授予其“中国象棋特级大师”称号，并授予“体育运动荣誉奖章”。1988 年胡荣华获得亚洲象棋联合会授予的“中国象棋国际特级大师”称号。

Hu Ronghua (1945-), born in Shanghai, master of Chinese chess, major founder of contemporary chess school and one of the most outstanding chess players in the 20th century, is called "Commander Hu" by the field of chess.

Hu Ronghua won the championship when he first attended national games at the age of 15, who then became the first-class player across China. He won individual champions in the Chinese Chess Games 14 times. From 1960 to 1979, he even created the miracle of winning ten consecutive champions. In 1982, he was awarded the title "Super Master of Chinese Chess" by the General Administration of Sport of China, alongside the "Sports Medal of Honor". In 1988, he was awarded the title "International Super Master of Chinese Chess" launched by the Asian Xiangqi Federation.

火箭队限量版 11号复古球衣

Limited Edition No.11 Retro Jersey of Houston Rockets

□ 本件球衣为复古款式，以红色为底色，领口和两侧以橙、白色线条装饰，正中有“Houston 11”字样。全球限量发行100件，上有姚明手写编号“46/100”。

□ 姚明（1980—），上海人，1998年4月入选国家队，司职中锋。在2002年NBA选秀中，他以状元秀身份加入NBA休斯敦火箭队，2003年至2008年连续6个赛季入选NBA西部全明星阵容。2011年7月20日，姚明宣布退役。2016年4月4日入选2016年奈·史密斯篮球名人纪念堂，成为首位获此殊荣的中国人。2017年2月23日当选为中国篮球协会主席，7月21日当选CBA董事长，2019年6月11日当选亚篮联主席。

□ The jersey is a retro style in a red background, with orange and white lines on the neckline and sides, with the words “Houston 11” in the front. There are only 100 pieces of this suit released worldwide, with Yao Ming handwritten number “46 / 100”.

□ Yao Ming (1980-), born in Shanghai, was selected as the national team in April 1998 and serves as a center. In the 2002 NBA Draft, he joined the NBA Houston Rockets as the NBA form dollar shows, and was selected to the NBA Western All-Star team for six consecutive seasons from 2003 to 2008. On July 20, 2011, Yao Ming announced his retirement. On April 4, 2016, he was elected into the 2016 Naismith Memorial Basketball Hall of Fame, becoming the first Chinese to win this honor. He was elected chairman of the Chinese Basketball Association on February 23, 2017, chairman of the CBA on July 21, and chairman of the Asian Basketball Federation (FIBA ASIA) on June 11, 2019.

尺寸 /Size：

48 码

捐赠者 /Donated by：

姚明 /Yao Ming

年代 /Date：

当代 /Contemporary

第一届
亚洲新兴力量运动会
奖牌

Medal of the 1st Sports Meet of the New Emerging Asian Forces

□ 奖牌表面錾刻有印度教、婆罗门教三大主神之一梵天的形象，背面为比赛名称、会徽、年份及举办地等信息，连接奖牌的坠子饰有山、火纹样，颇具宗教元素。

□ 1965 年 9 月 26 日，新运会亚洲委员会在北京成立。会议选举中国为执委会主席，决定 1966 年举办第一届亚洲新兴力量运动会。1966 年 11 月 25 日至 12 月 6 日，亚洲新兴力量运动会在柬埔寨首都金边举行。中国、日本、印度、印度尼西亚、朝鲜、越南等来自亚洲 17 个国家和地区的近 2 000 名运动员参加，中国派出以黄中为团长的 331 人组成的体育代表团赴会。本届运动会共设篮球、足球、排球、田径等 21 个正式比赛项目。中国体育代表团共获得 113 枚金牌、59 枚银牌和 36 枚铜牌。在举重、射击、田径、游泳等项目上，运动水平有较大提高，共有 2 人 2 次打破两项世界纪录，4 人 65 次打破 51 项新运会纪录，19 人 19 次打破 18 项全国纪录。

□ The surface of each medal is engraved with the image of Brahma, the King of Heaven and one of the three major gods of Hinduism and Brahmanism. The back is the name, the emblem, the year and the host place of the competition. The pendants connecting the medals are decorated with mountains and fire patterns, showing religious elements.

□ On September 26, 1965, the Asian Committee of the Sports Meet of the New Emerging Asian Forces was established in Beijing. China was elected presidency of the Executive Committee and the 1st Sports Meet of the New Emerging Asian Forces in 1966. From November 25 to December 6, 1966, the Sports Meet of New Emerging Asian Forces was held in Phnom Penh, capital of Cambodia. Nearly 2,000 athletes from 17 countries and regions in Asia, including China, Japan, India, Indonesia, DPR. Korea and Vietnam, etc. attended the event. China sent a sports delegation consisting of 331 people headed by Huang Zhong. The event set a total of 21 official sports, including basketball, soccer, volleyball and athletics. The Chinese sports delegation won 113 gold, 59 silver and 36 bronze medals. In terms of weight-lifting, shooting, athletics, swimming and other sports, Chinese athletes' competitiveness had been greatly improved, with 2 athletes breaking 2 world records twice, 4 athletes breaking 51 records of the event for 65 times and 19 athletes breaking 18 national records for 19 times.

尺寸 /Size：
Φ62mm × 4mm
重量 /Weight：
金 /Gold：117.7g
银 /Silver：115.7g
年代 /Date：
1966

第七届 伊朗德黑兰亚运会 佩章、纪念章

Badge and Commemorative Badge of the 7th Asian Games

□ 佩章、纪念章皆以黄、绿二色为主色调，章上以会徽为主要元素，外圈是亚运会名称及时间。

□ 1974 年 9 月 1—16 日，第七届亚运会在伊朗德黑兰召开，这是中国第一次参加亚洲运动会。亚洲 20 多个国家和地区的近 3 000 名运动员分别参加了 16 个项目的比赛。中国代表团中有 33 人来自上海。9 月 5 日，在女子标准手枪 25 米 60 发的比赛中，我国运动员李亚敏以 555 环的成绩，打破了澳大利亚运动员特里姆创造的 554 环的世界纪录。中国队居金牌总数第三。亚运会期间，9 个亚洲单项体育组织恢复了中华人民共和国有关单位体育组织的合法权利。

□ The two colors, yellow and green, are used as the main colors for both two badges. The emblem is the main element of the badge, and the outer ring is engraved with the name and time of the Asian Games.

□ From September 1 to 16, 1974, the 7th Asian Games was held in Tehran, Iran, which was the first time for China to participate in the Asian Games. Nearly 3,000 athletes from more than 20 countries and regions in Asia participated in 16 sports. A total of 33 members of the Chinese delegation came from Shanghai. On September 5, in the 25m 60-shot female standard pistol competition, Chinese athlete Li Yamin broke the world record of 554 rings created by Australian athlete Trim with the great achievement of 555 rings. China ranked third in terms of the total number of gold medals. During the Asian Games, nine Asian single sports organizations restored the legal rights of relevant institutions in the People's Republic of China to organize sports events.

佩章
Badge
尺寸 /Size：
Φ45mm × 3mm
绶带长 210mm
重量 /Weight：
43.8g
年代 /Date：
1974

纪念章
Commemorative Badge
尺寸 /Size:
Φ70mm × 8mm
重量 /Weight:
196.8g
年代 /Date:
1974

第五届全国运动会火炬

Torch of the 5th National Games

□ 本届全运会火炬表面呈银白色，火炬头部以五条几何状铁片承托，象征着第五届全运会，金色的球体连接手柄，造型简洁大方。

□ 1983 年，中华人民共和国第五届运动会在上海举行，这是第一次在北京以外的城市举办全运会，从此开启了全运会由不同城市举办的历史。国际奥委会前主席萨马兰奇出席了开幕式。这届全运会设田径、游泳、跳水、水球、体操、艺术体操、篮球、排球、足球、乒乓球、羽毛球、网球、手球、曲棍球、射击、射箭、举重、摔跤、柔道、击剑、自行车、赛艇、皮划艇、帆船、帆板 25 个比赛项目和 1 个表演项目（武术）。这届全运会上，共有 2 人 3 次破 2 项世界纪录，1 人 1 次破 1 项世界青年纪录，4 人 5 次平 3 项世界纪录，7 人 12 次破 9 项亚洲纪录，66 人 39 个队 145 次刷新 61 项全国纪录。上海代表团获得 33 枚金牌、35 枚银牌、30 枚铜牌，奖牌总数列全国第一，金牌数名列全国第二。上海运动员朱建华在预赛、决赛中两次打破男子跳高世界纪录，以满票当选为这届运动会“最受欢迎的运动员”。

□ The surface of the torch of this National Games is silver-white. The top of the torch is supported by five geometric iron sheets symbolizing the 5th National Games, and the golden ball is connected to the handle. The whole shape is simple and elegant.

□ In 1983, the 5th National Games of the People's Republic of China was held in Shanghai. It was the first time that the National Games was held in a city except Beijing. Since then, the National Games has been hosted in turn by different cities in China. The former IOC President Samaranch attended the opening ceremony at that time. The 5th National Games has 25 sporting events, including athletes, swimming, diving, water polo, gymnasium, rhythmic gymnastics, basketball, volleyball, football, table tennis, badminton, tennis, handball, field hockey, shooting, archery, weightlifting, wrestling, judo, fencing, bicycle, rowing, canoe sprint, sailing, and windsurfing as well as 1 performing event (martial arts). At this National Games, 2 athletes broke 2 world records for 3 times, 1 broke 1 world youth record for one time, 4 equaled 3 world records for 5 times, 7 broke 9 Asian records for 12 times, and 66 athletes from 39 teams rewrote 61 national records for 145 times. The delegation team of Shanghai won 33 gold medals, 35 silver medals and 30 copper medals. The total number of medals ranked the first and the number of gold medals ranked the second domestically. Zhu Jianhua, a high jumper from Shanghai, broke the world record respectively in the preliminary and final contests, thus was elected as the "most popular athlete" of this Games by a unanimous vote.

尺寸 /Size:
Φ197mm × 845mm
重量 /Weight:
2 093.7g
年代 /Date:
1983

第五届全国运动会国画

Chinese painting themed on the opening of the 5th National Games

□ 1983 年 9 月 18 日至 10 月 1 日，第五届全国运动会在上海召开，这是第一次在首都以外的城市举办全运会，并开始按奥运会的竞赛项目设置。为了庆祝这一盛事，上海画坛十几位大师欢聚在上海市体育俱乐部，挥毫泼墨，共绘良辰美景表示庆贺。参加这一活动合作作画的上海著名画家有：唐云、朱屺瞻、沈迈士、万籁鸣、钱君匋、应野平、黄幻吾、吴青霞、陈佩秋、薛佛影、赵宏本、戚叔玉、糜耕云。上海著名画家王个簃为此幅难得的画作题词：笔飞墨舞心情畅，万紫千红景色新；拼搏精神扬正气，百花竞艳共迎春。

□ From September 18 to October 1, 1983, the 5th National Games was held in Shanghai. This was the first time that the National Games was held in a city other than the Capital, and it began to be set up according to the competition items of the Olympic Games. In order to celebrate this event, more than a dozen masters from the Shanghai painting circle gathered at the Shanghai Sports Club, splashing ink and painting together, including Tang Yun, Zhu Qizhan, Shen Maishi, Wan Laiming, Qian Juntao, Ying Yeping, Huang Huanwu, Wu Qingxia, Chen Peiqiu, Xue Foying, Zhao Hongben, Qi Shuyu, Mi Gengyun. The famous Shanghai painter Wang Geyi wrote the title for this rare painting "The flowing calligraphy revealing smooth mood, the blaze of bright colors showing beautiful scenery. The spirit of struggle promoting uprightness, blooming flowers welcoming the spring".

笔飞墨舞心情畅，
万紫千红景色新。
拼搏精神扬正气，
百花竞艳共迎春。

第五届全运会在上海胜利召开，
合作此画于政协上海市委员会
唐云、朱屺瞻、沈迈士、
万籁鸣、钱君匋、应野平、
黄幻吾、吴青霞、陈佩秋、
薛佛影、赵宏本、戚叔玉、
糜耕云合作
王个簃并题
一九八三年九月

尺寸 /Size:
4 420mm × 1 620mm
年代 /Date:
1983

第一届
东亚运动会
火炬、火种盒

Torch and tinderbox of the 1st East Asian Games

□ 火炬整体围绕“太阳”而设计，在喷火口周围有太阳燃烧火团图案，下方有本届运动会会徽，火炬中段由一个橙色球体连接，球体上绘有 9 个相交的圆环，代表 9 个参赛国家和地区，手柄表面有白玉兰图案，代表东道主上海。

□ 火种盒外形为圆形盒式，呈银白色，上面标有“神州 Shenzhou”字样。

□ The torch takes a shape of round box surrounding the “sun”, with a silver-white surface. There is a pattern of burning sun around the flame vent. The emblem of the Games is on the top of the torch, and below the emblem is a sphere made of nine rings connected with one another, representing nine countries and regions taking part in the Games. There is a pattern of Magnolia denudata on the surface of its handle, representing the host city, Shanghai.

□ The tinderbox takes a shape of silver-white round box, marked with two Chinese characters “Shenzhou”.

尺寸 /Size:
Φ235mm × 150mm
重量 /Weight:
4 708g
年代 /Date:
1993

尺寸 /Size：
Φ197mm × 560mm
重量 /Weight：
1 900g
年代 /Date：
1993

第一届
东亚运动会
金、银、铜牌
Gold, Silver and Bronze Medals from the 1st East Asian Games

□ 奖牌内圈刻有本届东亚运动会会徽，由英文“East Asian”（东亚）的第一个字母“E”和阿拉伯数字“1”组成，表示第一届东亚运动会。“E”和“1”组成汉字“申”，象征第一届东亚运动会在中国上海举行。红色的“E”表示强烈，给人以燃烧的火炬的形象，同时又似运动中的人体。外圈上是中英文的“上海第一届东亚运动会”字样。

□ 1993年5月9—18日，第一届东亚运动会在上海举行，这是上海在全国率先尝试由地方政府承办国际综合性运动会。中国、日本、蒙古、朝鲜、韩国和中国香港、中国澳门、中国台北等8个国家和地区及关岛（特邀代表团）参加了本届东亚运动会。共有1 252名运动员参加了田径、游泳、篮球、足球、保龄球、拳击、羽毛球、柔道、举重、武术、体操、赛艇12个项目的比赛。网球作为表演项目列入。中国获奖牌213枚（金牌105枚、银牌74枚、铜牌34枚），日本获奖牌117枚（金牌25枚、银牌37枚、铜牌55枚），韩国获奖牌91枚（金牌23枚、银牌28枚、铜牌40枚），分列前三名。并有7人14次打破13项亚洲纪录。

□ The inner circle of the medal is engraved with the emblem of the 1993 East Asian Games. It is composed of the letter “E” and Arabic number “1”, representing the first East Asian Games. “E” and “1” constitute the Chinese characters “ 申 ”(pronounced as “shen”) which symbolizes that the first East Asian Games was held in Shanghai, China. The red “E” looks powerful, reminding people of a burning torch, and it looks like a body in motion. The outer ring is marked with the words “Shanghai 1st East Asian Games” in Chinese and English.

□ From May 9 to 18, 1993, the first East Asian Games was held in Shanghai, which was an attempt by Shanghai to host an international comprehensive sports event by the local government for the first time nationwide. Eight countries and regions including China, Japan, Mongolia, DPR. Korea, Republic of Korea, Hong Kong region, Macao region and Chinese Taipei as well as Guam (specially invited delegation) participated in this East Asian Games. A total of 1,252 athletes participated in 12 events, including athletics, swimming, basketball, football, bowling, boxing, badminton, judo, weightlifting, wushu, gymnastics and rowing. Tennis was included as a demonstration sports. China won 213 medals (105 gold, 74 silver and 34 bronze); Japan won 117 medals (25 gold, 37 silver and 55 bronze); and ROK won 91 medals (23 gold, 28 silver and 40 bronze). They ranked top three. Seven people broke 13 Asian records 14 times.

尺寸 /Size：
Φ55mm×5mm
重量 /Weight：
金 /Gold：113g
银 /Silver：108.4g
铜 /Bronze：96.3g
年代 /Date：
1993

第八届
全国运动会
火炬、火种盒

Torches and tinderbox of the 8th National Games

□ 火炬通体为金色、银色。火炬头部圆柱上有 8 条装饰筋，一是取意八运会的“8”字，二是寓意火炬传递是一项全民健身、八方参与的活动。火炬头部设计酷似一个齿轮，寄意中国工业将有新的腾飞。火炬正面有第八届全运会的会徽图案。

□ 第八届全运会火种盒由 52 个零件组成，外形为圆形盒式，呈银白色，上面标有八运会标志。结构上采用了现代化技术，燃烧时火焰呈金黄色，有很强的抗风、抗雨能力。

□ The whole body of the torches are golden and silvery. There are 8 decorative ribs on the column top of the torch. Such a design firstly means the “8th” time for which the National Games of the People’s Republic of China was held and secondly implies that the torch relay is an activity involving the people from all walks of life. The head of the torch is designed to look like a gear, implying that China’s industry will see a new rise. Its front is printed with the emblem of the 8th National Games.

□ The silver-white kindling box is composed of 52 parts, taking a shape of round box and marked with the emblem of the 8th National Games. The structure adopts modern technology, the flame is golden yellow, and it has strong wind rain resistance.

尺寸 /Size：
Φ250mm × 175mm
重量 /Weight：
3 406g
年代 /Date：
1997

尺寸 /Size:
Φ125mm × 510mm
重量 /Weight:
1 900g
年代 /Date:
1997

世界乒乓球锦标赛奖牌

Medals from World Table Tennis Championships

□ 世乒赛奖牌多以圆形为主，有少量方形及星形奖牌，奖牌的设计皆由世乒赛主办国承担，多枚奖牌上运用了乒乓的元素。

□ 世界乒乓球锦标赛简称“世乒赛”，每届比赛由国际乒乓球联合会授权比赛地乒乓球协会主办，具有广泛的影响力。始于 1926 年，每年举办一次，从 1959 年的第二十五届开始改为每两年举办一次。与乒乓球世界杯、奥运会并称为“乒乓球运动的三大赛事”。分为男子单打、女子单打、男子双打、女子双打、男子团体、女子团体、混合双打 7 项赛事。

□ Most medals of the World Table Tennis Championships are round, the minority of them are shaped like squares or stars. The design of the medals was undertaken by the host countries of the championships, and the elements of table tennis were used on many medals.

□ Every session of the World Table Tennis Championships was hosted by the table tennis society in the place authorized by the International Table Tennis Federation (ITTF), which is of profound influence. Dating back to 1926, it was held once a year, while it was held every two years since the 25th session in 1959. Alongside with the Table Tennis World Cup and the Olympic Games, they were called “three big events of table tennis”. There were seven competitions: men’s and women’s single, double and mixed and men’s and women’s team.

尺寸 /Size:
35mm × 50mm × 2mm
重量 /Weight:
19g
年代 /Date:
1961

尺寸 /Size:
Φ55mm × 4mm
重量 /Weight:
75.5g
年代 /Date:
1963

尺寸 /Size:
Φ60mm × 5mm
重量 /Weight:
135.2g
年代 /Date:
1971

尺寸 /Size:
Φ88mm × 4mm
重量 /Weight:
245.4g
年代 /Date:
1973

尺寸 /Size:
Φ65mm × 3mm
重量 /Weight:
99.1g
年代 /Date:
1975

尺寸 /Size:
Φ60mm × 3mm
重量 /Weight:
84.5g
年代 /Date:
1977

尺寸 /Size:
Φ62mm × 5mm
重量 /Weight:
123g
年代 /Date:
1979

尺寸 /Size:
Φ70mm × 3mm
重量 /Weight:
119.5g
年代 /Date:
1981

尺寸 /Size:
Φ70mm × 5mm
重量 /Weight:
182.5g
年代 /Date:
1983

尺寸 /Size:
70mm × 50mm × 3mm
重量 /Weight:
98.1g
年代 /Date:
1985

尺寸 /Size:
Φ65mm × 4mm
重量 /Weight:
127.3g
年代 /Date:
1987

尺寸 /Size:
Φ70mm × 4mm
重量 /Weight:
183.3g
年代 /Date:
1989

尺寸 /Size:
Φ70mm × 6mm
重量 /Weight:
187g
年代 /Date:
1991

尺寸 /Size:
50mm × 70mm × 3mm
重量 /Weight:
95.7g
年代 /Date:
1993

尺寸 /Size:
Φ60mm × 4mm
重量 /Weight:
130g
年代 /Date:
1995

尺寸 /Size:
Φ70mm × 5mm
重量 /Weight:
157.1g
年代 /Date:
1997

尺寸 /Size:
Φ62mm × 3mm
重量 /Weight:
121.6g
年代 /Date:
1999

第四十八届
世界乒乓球锦标赛
金、银、铜牌

Gold, Silver and Bronze Medals from the 48th World Table Tennis Championships

□ 奖牌中间有第 48 届世乒赛会徽以及上海外滩的标志性剪影，外圈刻有比赛名称、时间及举办地。

□ 2005 年 4 月 30 日至 5 月 6 日，第 48 届世乒赛在上海举行，这是继 1961 年北京世乒赛、1995 年天津世乒赛后，中国作为东道主第三次承办的乒坛盛会。共有 147 个国家和地区的 1 500 名运动员、教练员、官员参加了本次世乒赛。中国选手包揽全部 5 个单项的冠军。王励勤、张怡宁分获男女单打冠军；孔令辉、王皓和王楠、张怡宁分获男女双打冠军；王励勤、郭跃获得混双冠军。

□ In the middle of the medal is the emblem of the 48th World Table Tennis Championships and the iconic silhouette of Shanghai Bund. The name, time and venue of the competition are engraved on the outer ring.

□ From April 30 to May 6, 2005, the 48th World Table Tennis Championships was held in Shanghai. This is the third grand table tennis event hosted by China after the 1961 World Table Tennis Championships in Beijing and 1995 Championships in Tianjin. A total of 1,500 athletes, coaches and officials from 147 countries and regions participated in the championships. The Chinese contestants won all five individual championships. Wang Liqin and Zhang Yining won the champions of men's and women's singles respectively; Kong Linghui and Wang Hao won the champion of men's double while Wang Nan and Zhang Yining won the champion of women's double; Wang Liqin and Guo Yue won the champion of mixed double.

尺寸 /Size：
Φ80mm × 4mm
重量 /Weight：
金 /Gold：195.9g
银 /Silver：196.6g
铜 /Bronze：202.8g
年代 /Date：
2005

国际泳联世界杯短池游泳系列赛上海站金、银、铜牌

FINA Swimming World Cup Shanghai (China) Medal

□ 奖牌呈长方形，上方刻有国际泳联的缩写“Fina”和会徽图案，下刻有“Swimming World Cup 2002-2003”的字样及举办地“Shanghai”和时间“1-2 December 2003”。

□ 世界杯短池游泳系列赛是一个国际系列短池（25 米）游泳比赛，由国际泳联主办，参赛成员是国际泳联会员。该系列比赛于 1989 年开始，每年举办分站的比赛，最终获得前三名的运动员可以获得奖金。2002—2003 年世界杯短池游泳系列赛分 3 个赛区（美洲区、亚太区和欧洲区）7 站（里约热内卢、纽约、上海、墨尔本、巴黎、斯德哥尔摩、柏林）进行，上海承办第三站比赛。这是上海举办的又一项世界性赛事。为了确保比赛的高水平，国际泳联推出一系列新的措施，其中包括将每一个分站的奖金提高至 6 万美元，总奖金高达 66 万美元，并规定设立分站的国家必须派出一流选手参赛。

□ The medal is rectangular. It is engraved with the abbreviation “FINA” of the Fédération Internationale de Natation Association and the FINA emblem engraved on the top, with the words “Swimming World Cup 2002-2003”, the location “Shanghai” and the time of the event “1-2 December 2003” on the back.

□ The World Cup Short Pool Swimming Series is an international series of short pool (25m) swimming competition sponsored by FINA and participating members are FINA members.The series began in 1989, with annual competition, and the top three finalists can receive prize money. The 2002-2003 FINA Swimming World Cup Series was held at 7 stations (Rio de Janeiro, New York, Shanghai, Melbourne, Paris, Stockholm and Berlin) in three regions (America, Asia Pacific and Europe), and Shanghai hosted the third competition. This is also another world event held in Shanghai. In order to ensure a high-level competition, FINA has launched a series of new measures, including raising the bonus of each station to USD 60,000, with a total bonus of up to USD 660,000, and making it a rule that countries serving as stations must send first-class players to participate in the competition.

尺寸 /Size：
50mm × 100mm × 5mm
重量 /Weight：
金 /Gold：112g
银 /Silver：112.7g
铜 /Bronze：115.7g
年代 /Date：
2003

第十四届国际泳联世界游泳锦标赛金、银、铜牌

Gold, Silver and Bronze Medals from the 14th FINA World Championships

□ 奖牌中间是第十四届锦标赛的会徽，会徽造型为地球形泳帽背景下代表“上海”的英文字母“S”和 2011 数字构成的图案，整体外形如同在水面上劈波斩浪、奋勇拼搏的泳坛健儿，外圈上方以水滴形装饰，下方写有“第 14 届国际泳联世界锦标赛上海 2011”的字样。

□ 世界游泳锦标赛是由国际泳联主办的最高级别的大型国际性游泳赛事，包括游泳、跳水、花样游泳、水球、公开水域 5 个大项。2011 年 7 月 16—31 日，第十四届世界游泳锦标赛在上海举行，这是国际泳联世锦赛首度落户中国，也是继2001年日本福冈之后，第二次在亚洲举办这一大赛。本届世锦赛，中国队共获得 15 金、13 银、8 铜。其中，由吴敏霞领衔的中国跳水“梦之队”包揽了该项目全部 10 块金牌。

□ In the middle of the medal is the emblem of the 14th Championships, which is a pattern composed of the English letter “S” representing “Shanghai” and the number 2011 against the background of a globe-shaped swimming cap. On the whole, it looks like a swimmer cleaving through the waves in a fighting spirit. The upper part of the outer ring is decorated with a water drop shape, and the words “14th FINA World Championship Shanghai 2011” are written on the lower part.

□ The FINA World Championships is the highest-level large-scale international swimming event sponsored by the FINA General Association. It includes five major events, namely swimming, diving, synchronized swimming, water polo and open water. From July 16 to 31, 2011, the 14th FINA World Championships was held in Shanghai. This is the first time that the FINA World Championships was held in China, and it is also the second time this competition has been held in Asia after the competition held in Fukuoka, Japan in 2001. At this world championships, the Chinese team won 15 gold, 13 silver and 8 bronze medals. Among them, the Chinese Diving Team known as the “Dream Team” led by Wu Minxia achieved a clean sweep of all the ten gold medals of the diving competition.

尺寸 /Size：
Φ70mm × 5mm
重量 /Weight：
金 /Gold：219.3g
银 /Silver：215.3g
铜 /Bronze：218.9g
年代 /Date：
2011

第十八届国际篮联篮球世界杯国际篮联官员签名篮球

Basketball with the autographs of FIBA top officials from the 18th FIBA Basketball World Cup

篮球上有国际篮联主席霍拉西奥·穆拉托雷、国际篮联秘书长安德里亚·扎格里斯、国际篮联副主席哈玛尼·尼昂的签名。篮球中间绘有本届篮球世界杯会徽和“2019 年上海篮球世界杯”的英文字样，以及上海的标志性建筑东方明珠电视塔和“举办城市上海”的英文字样。同时印有“中国龙”纹样，并加入了“心”“篮筐”“球”“球场”四大篮球世界杯品牌元素。

2019 年 8 月 31 日至 9 月 15 日，第十八届国际篮联篮球世界杯（2019 FIBA Basketball World Cup）在中国的上海和北京、广州、南京、武汉、深圳、佛山、东莞八座城市举行。参赛队伍 32 支。上海赛区的比赛在东方体育中心进行，承担了 E 组美国、土耳其、捷克、日本的 6 场小组比赛和 4 场排名赛、2 场四分之一决赛、1 场 5~8 名排名赛。

The basketball is with the signatures of Holacio Muratore, President of the International Basketball Federation, Andria Zagres, Secretary-General of the International Basket Federation, and Hamani Nyon, Vice-President of the International Basket Federation. The middle of the basketball is painted with the emblem of the Basketball World Cup and the English words of “Shanghai Basketball World Cup 2019”, as well as the pattern of “The Shanghai Oriental Pearl & TV Tower”, the landmark building of Shanghai, and the English words “The Host City, Shanghai”. At the same time, the pattern of “Chinese dragon” is printed on it, and four major brand elements of the Basketball World Cup of “heart”, “basket”, “ball” and “pitch” are added.

From August 31 to September 15, 2019, the 18th FIBA Basketball World Cup was held in Shanghai and eight cities in China, including Beijing, Guangzhou, Nanjing, Wuhan, Shenzhen, Foshan and Dongguan. And there were 32 teams. The Shanghai competition was held in the Oriental Sports Center, and it undertook six team competitions and four rankings competitions, two quarter finals competitions and one 5~8 rankings competitions in Group E of America, Turkey, Czech Republic and Japan.

尺寸 /Size:
Φ246mm
年代 /Date:
2019

第十五届世界武术锦标赛金、银、铜牌

Gold, Silver and Bronze Medals from the 15th World Wushu Championships

□ 奖牌采用“金”与“汉白玉”的元素，体现玉之五德。表面以上海特有的石库门造型为轮廓，下方以浦江沿岸外滩建筑为剪影，海派风情与武术精神相辅相成。

□ 世界武术锦标赛由国际武术联合会主办，每两年举行一届，各武术会员国轮流举办，是世界武术界最高级别的国际大赛。2019 年 10 月 19—23 日，第十五届世界武术锦标赛在上海举行，来自 102 个国家和地区约 1 100 余名运动员、教练员、裁判员、官员和嘉宾参加了大赛。比赛分为套路和散打，套路比赛包括男子、女子共 26 个项目，散打比赛包括男子、女子共 18 个项目。每个国家或地区限报 1 支参赛队（限报 24 人）。每支参赛队组成：1 组套路队（限报 12 人）和 1 组散打队（限报 12 人）。中国队摘获 14 金 1 银 1 铜，排在金牌榜和奖牌榜首位。伊朗获得 9 金 2 银 1 铜排第二位，中国香港获得 5 金 4 银 1 铜排第三位。

□ The medal is based on gold and white marble, reflecting the five virtues of jade. The upper part of the jade is contoured by the unique Shikumen scenic spot of Shanghai while the lower part looks like the silhouette of the buildings on the Bund along the Huangpu River. The Shanghai style and the spirit of martial arts complement each other.

□ The World Wushu Championships sponsored by the International Wushu Federation held every two years by all member states in turn is a top-level international competition in the wushu community around the world. From October 19 to 23, 2019, the 15th World Wushu Championship was held in Shanghai, with over 1,100 athletes, coaches, referees, officials and guests from 102 countries and regions participating in the event. The competition includes martial arts repertoire and free combat. The repertoire includes 26 competitions for men and women while the free combat includes 18 events for men and women. Each country or region is limited to send 1 team (limited to 24 players) for the competition. The composition of each participating team: 1 group of repertoire team (limited to 12 players) and 1 group of free combat team (limited to 12 players). The Chinese team won 14 gold, 1 silver and 1 bronze medals, ranking first in the gold medal standings and medal count. Iran won second place with 9 gold, 2 silver and 1 bronze medals, and Hong Kong won third place with 5 gold, 4 silver and 1 bronze medals.

尺寸 /Size：
Φ70×5mm
重量 /Weight：
金 /Gold：171.9g
银 /Silver：171g
铜 /Bronze：171.7g
年代 /Date：
2019

上海国际马拉松赛20年奖牌

The 20th anniversary medal of Shanghai International Marathon

□ This is the first medal inlaid with real gold in the history of the Shanghai International Marathon. Streamlines are used to symbolize the marathon track while “Twenty years of Shanghai International Marathon” are engraved on a pure gold medal. On the back of the medal is marked “42.195 km” for the full length of the marathon and “2015.11.8” (November 8, 2015) for the time.

□ 这是上海国际马拉松赛历史上第一枚镶有真金的奖牌，用流线型线条演绎马拉松跑道，以足金金章带出“二十年，跑向前”的目标。奖牌背面有马拉松全长“42.195km”和时间“2015.11.8”的标记。

尺寸 /Size:
60mm × 90mm × 7mm
重量 /Weight:
144g
年代 /Date:
2015

上海国际马拉松赛于 1996 年创办，每年 11 月底举行，参赛者来自世界五大洲 42 个国家和地区以及中国 34 个省级行政区的马拉松选手和路跑爱好者。比赛项目设男、女全程马拉松（42.195 公里），男、女半程马拉松（21.0975 公里），健身跑（5 公里），2013 年起新增 10 公里跑项目。2020 年 3 月，上海国际马拉松赛获得“世界田径白金赛事”称号。已经逐渐成为上海城市的一个名片和市民的节日。

The Shanghai International Marathon was started in 1996 and held at the end of November each year. Participants are marathon runners and road runners from 42 countries and regions on five continents in the world and 34 provincial administrative regions in China.The competition events include male and female full marathons (42.195 km), male and female half marathons (21.0975 km) and fitness races (5 km). Since 2013, a new 10 km running competition has been added. In March 2020, the Shanghai International Marathon was awarded the title of World Athletics Platinum Race. It has gradually become a business card and a festival for residents in Shanghai.

首届 F1 中国大奖赛裁判装备

Referee cap and uniform for the 1st F1 Chinese Grand Prix

☐ 裁判服以红色为主，胸口印有本届大奖赛的会徽。帽子是黑色装饰，有红色花纹，正前方印有会徽及比赛名称。

☐ 世界一级方程式锦标赛（简称 F1），是由国际汽车运动联合会（FIA）举办的最高等级的年度系列场地赛车比赛，是当今世界最高水平的赛车比赛，与奥运会、世界杯足球赛并称为“世界三大体育盛事”，2004 年进入上海，在上海国际赛车场举行，上海国际赛道的总长度为 5 451.24 米，具有 7 处左转弯道及 7 处右转弯道。法拉利车队的巴里切罗以 1 小时 29 分 12 秒 42 的成绩获得了中国站的第一个冠军。英美车队的巴顿获得亚军，迈凯轮梅赛德斯车队的莱库宁获得季军。F1 中国大奖赛到 2019 年已连续成功举办 16 年。2019 年 F1 中国大奖赛成为 F1 历史上第 1 000 站大奖赛，赛事的商业运作和办赛质量不断提升，赢得了国内外各界的高度赞誉和评价。

☐ The referee uniform is in red with the emblem of the competition printed on the chest. The black referee hat is decorated with red patterns. At the center of the front are printed with the emblem and name of the competition.

☐ FIA Formula 1 World Championship, usually called F1 for short, refers to the highest-level annual series of track racing competitions held by Fédération Internationale de l'Automobile (FIA). As a racing competition of the highest degree in the world today, F1 is included into “Three Major Word Sports” with the Olympic Games and FIFA World Cup. F1 was introduced into Shanghai in 2004 and held in Shanghai International Circuit which covers a total length of 5,451.24 meters with 7 left turns and 7 right turns. In the competition, Rubens Barrichello from Scuderia Mission Winnow Ferrari won the first championship with a result of 1 hour, 29 minutes and 12.42 seconds. Jenson Button from British American Racing won the second prize, and Kimi Raikkonen from McLaren-Mercedes F1 Team won the third prize. Since 2019, Formula 1 Chinese Grand Prix has been held for 16 consecutive years. The competition in 2019 marks the 1,000th Grand Prix of F1 in history. Thanks to the continuous improvement in commercial operation and competition quality, Formula 1 Chinese Grand Prix has won wide praise and appreciation from home and abroad.

尺寸 /Size：
裁判服 /Referee uniform：
L 码
裁判帽 /Referee cup：
280mm × 230mm
年代 /Date：
2004

NBA 中国赛球队签名篮球

Autographed basketball from the NBA China Games

□ 篮球印有休斯敦火箭队及萨克拉门托国王队的队徽，队徽间有“VS.”的字样，表面有 NBA 球员签名。

□ NBA 季前赛于 2004 年首次登陆中国。2007 年、2012—2017 年都在上海举办过季前赛。NBA 中国赛逐渐成了一项常规化的赛事，而一系列的 NBA 球队来到中国打球，也为扩展 NBA 在中国的市场，起到了相当积极的作用。2004 年 10 月 14 日和 17 日，NBA 中国赛分别在上海和北京举行，对阵双方是 NBA 休斯敦火箭队和萨克拉门托国王队。14 日上海站比赛，休斯敦火箭队以 88 比 86 击败萨克拉门托国王队。其中火箭队此役 5 人得分上双，姚明拿下 14 分、7 个篮板。

□ On the surface of the basketball are printed with the team emblems of Houston Rockets and Sacramento Kings, during which there is a “VS.” and signatures of the NBA players.

□ NBA pioneered its preseason in China in 2004. More NBA preseason games were held in Shanghai in 2007 and between 2012 and 2017. As NBA China Games were getting more regular, a series of NBA teams came to China for the games, which expanded the share of NBA in the Chinese market. On October 14 and 17, 2004, the NBA China Games were held in Shanghai and Beijing respectively. The competing side is the Houston Rockets and Sacramento Kings. On October 14 in Shanghai, Houston Rockets defeated Sacramento Kings 88∶86. 5 players in Houston Rockets won double scores. Yao Ming gained 14 scores and 7 rebounds.

尺寸 /Size:
7 号
年代 /Date:
2004

NBA 总冠军戒指
NBA Championship Rings

□ 戒面呈方形样式，银质，表面近百颗白色皓石镶嵌在绿色皓石组成的三叶草外，象征着本届冠军队伍凯尔特人，戒面两端刻有“WORLD CHAMPIONS”字样。戒指侧面一面刻有凯尔特人 5 号球员加内特（Garnett）的名字，另一面刻有凯尔特人在 2008 年取得的战绩。

□ 2008 年 NBA 总决赛由东部联盟冠军波士顿凯尔特人队与西部联盟冠军洛杉矶湖人队对决。最终，波士顿凯尔特人队以 4 比 2 击败洛杉矶湖人队，获得了队史第 17 个 NBA 总冠军。

□ The silver ring is in a square shape with a hundred grains of white Zircon inlaid in the Shamrock made from green Zircon, symbolizing the championship team of Celtic. On the double sides of the ring are engraved with “WORLD CHAMPIONS”, the other side is engraved with what Boston Celtics achieved in 2008.

□ In the 2008 NBA Finals, Boston Celtics, the Eastern Conference champion, faced off against Los Angeles Lakers, the Western Conference champion. In the end, Boston Celtics defeated Los Angeles Lakers in 4-2 and won the 17th NBA championship trophy in team history.

尺寸 /Size:
戒面 /Ring Face:
25mm × 25mm
指宽 /Ring Diameter:
Φ30mm
重量 /Weight:
26g
年代 /Date:
2008

□ 戒面呈圆形，足金，中间刻有湖人队名称及冠军奖杯图案，外圈有“2009 World Champions”字样。戒指侧面一面刻有湖人队球员科比·布莱恩特（Bryant）的名字和头像，以及湖人队 2009 年 65 胜 17 负的战绩，另一面刻有湖人队打入总决赛和在总决赛上的比分。

□ 2009 年 NBA 总决赛由东部联盟冠军奥兰多魔术队与西部联盟冠军洛杉矶湖人队对决。最终，洛杉矶湖人队以 4 比 1 轻取奥兰多魔术队，捧起了队史第 15 座总冠军奖杯。科比·布莱恩特场均 32.4 分 5.6 篮板 7.4 助攻，生涯首次当选 FMVP。

□ The gold ring is in a round shape with the name of Lakers and the pattern of the championship Trophy engraved in the center and “2009 World Champions” on the outside. The side of the ring is engraved with the name and head of Los Angeles Lakers player Kobe(Bryant) and the Los Angeles Lakers' record of 65 wins and 17 losses in 2009 on one side and the Los Angeles Lakers' finals appearance and score in the finals on the other.

□ In the 2009 NBA Finals, Orlando Magic, the Eastern Conference champion, faced off against Los Angeles Lakers, the Western Conference champion. In the end, Los Angeles Lakers defeated Orlando Magic in 4-1 and won the 15th NBA championship trophy in the team history. Kobe Bryant averaged 32.4 points, 5.6 rebounds and 7.4 assists and won the first FMVP in his career.

尺寸 /Size:
戒面 /Ring Face:
Φ25mm
指宽 /Ring Diameter:
Φ32mm
重量 /Weight:
22.1g
年代 /Date:
2009

赛用
签名跑鞋
Autographed competition running shoe

□ 跑鞋曾为短跑运动员尤塞恩·博尔特使用。跑鞋为一只红色钉鞋，外侧印有品牌标志，前方写有博尔特签名。附 JSA 国际认证书。

□ 尤塞恩·博尔特（1985—），牙买加著名短跑运动员，绰号“闪电”，2008、2012、2016 年奥运会男子 100 米、200 米冠军，男子 100 米、200 米世界纪录保持者。2017 年 8 月 14 日，在 2017 年世界田径锦标赛赛后，博尔特正式宣布退役。

□ The running shoe was used by sprinter Usain Bolt. It is a red spiked shoe with the brand logo printed on the outside and the signature of Bolt on the front. an International certification of JSA attached.

□ Usain Bolt (1985-) is a famous Jamaican sprinter, nicknamed "Lightning". He won the gold medal in 100m and 200m Men Racing respectively in 2008, 2012 and 2016 Olympic Games. He is also the record holder of 100m, 200m Men Racing. On August 14, 2017, Bolt officially announced his retirement after the 2017 World Championships in Athletics.

尺寸 /Size：
US13、EUR47.5
年代 /Date：
2010

捶丸

A set of Chuiwan

□ 捶丸，顾名思义，捶者打也，丸者球也，是我国古代球戏之一。它的出现并盛行与唐代球类活动有密切的关系。唐代有一种拿球杆徒步击打的游戏，叫作“步打球”。唐代诗人王建在《宫词》第十三首中“寒食宫人步打球”，说的就是捶丸。到了宋朝，步打球由原来的同场对抗性竞赛逐渐演变为依次击球的非对抗性比赛，球门改为球穴，名称也随之改称“捶丸”。捶丸发展至明代，个别皇帝雅好此道，遂将捶丸引入宫中。现藏故宫博物院的明代《宣宗行乐图》长卷中，有一部分描绘的就是捶丸。后来在苏格兰出现的现代高尔夫，其形制、运动规则与我国的古代捶丸有着惊人的相似，显然具有源与流的关系，而捶丸的历史记述比高尔夫球的出现还要早 472 年。

□ As the name implies, “chui” means batting while “wan” means the ball. It is one of the ancient ball games in China. Its appearance and prevalence are closely related to ball games in the Tang Dynasty, during which there was a game of hitting the ball on foot called “batting on foot”. In the thirteenth poem of “Palace Verse”, the poet Wang Jian of the Tang Dynasty said “the palace people played batting on foot on the Cold Food Festival”, which was exactly talking about Chuiwan. In the Song Dynasty, the game of batting on foot gradually evolved from the original adversarial game of the same field to a non-adversarial game of successive shots. The goal was changed to a hole, and the name was subsequently changed into “Chuiwan”. In the Ming Dynasty, some emperors loved to play Chuiwan and introduced this game into the palace. A scenario in the long volume of Emperor Xuanzong in Pleasure now collected in the Palace Museum is about the Chuiwan game (golf in ancient China). The modern golf later appeared in Scotland is much like the Chuiwan game in ancient China in terms of shape and rules, for which one must be the source and the other descendant. According to historical records, Chuiwan is invented 472 years earlier than golf.

尺寸 /Size:
Φ25mm—Φ60mm
数量 /Amount:
12
年代 /Date:
唐至明代 /Tang Dynasty to Ming Dynasty
618 AD to 1644 AD

高尔夫球杆

Golf clubs

□ 本套球杆共有8支，杆头皆为金属制，另有一个帆布球杆套，用以装带球杆。

□ 15世纪高尔夫运动发源于苏格兰，当时的杆头由木头制成，苹果木、梨木、核桃木等皆可制成杆头。20世纪初，钢以其韧性强的优点取代了木头成为常见的杆头材质。

□ A set includes eight mallets whose head are made of metal and a canvas mallet cover.

□ Golf originated from Scotland in 1400s, when the mallets were made of wood, either apple wood, pear wood or walnut wood. In early 1900s, steel took the place of wood as the common material of mallet thanks to its toughness.

尺寸 /Size:
长 /Length:
950~1 200mm,
杆头宽 /Width:
38~55mm,
数量 /Amount:
一套 8 根
8 pieces/ set
年代 /Date:
近代 /Modern times

斯诺克选手签名球和球杆

Players-autographed Snooker Balls and Cue

□ 这是世界著名斯诺克选手签名的球和球杆。

□ 斯诺克球签名选手有：约翰·希金斯、尼尔·罗伯逊、斯蒂芬·李、彼得·艾伯顿、马克·威廉姆斯、马克·艾伦、肖恩·墨菲、阿里斯特·卡特、斯蒂芬·马奎尔、马丁·古尔德、巴里·霍金斯、弗盖里·奥布莱恩、斯图亚特·宾汉姆、格雷姆·多特。

□ 斯诺克球杆签名选手有：斯蒂芬·亨得利、罗尼·奥沙利文、贾德·特鲁姆普、约翰·希金斯、尼尔·罗伯逊、斯蒂芬·李、马库斯·坎贝尔、马克·威廉姆斯、马克·艾伦、肖恩·墨菲、阿里斯特·卡特、斯蒂芬·马奎尔、马丁·古尔德、里奇·沃顿、弗盖里·奥布莱恩、斯图亚特·宾汉姆、多米尼克·戴尔。

□ 斯诺克大师赛2007年登陆上海，是世界斯诺克职业巡回赛的官方排名赛，与世锦赛、英锦赛并称为世界三大赛。上海大师赛被世界台联称为海外赛事第一品牌，是中国境内举办的历史最悠久同时也是影响力最深远的顶级斯诺克赛事之一。2013年，中国选手丁俊晖夺得冠军。

□ This is a set of balls and a cue signed by world famous snooker players.

□ The players who signed are John Higgins, Neil Alexander Robertson, Stephen Lee, Peter Ebdon, Mark Williams, Mark Allen, Shaun Murphy, Allister Carter, Stephen Maguire, Martin Gould, Barry Hawkins, Fergal O'Brien, Stuart Bingham and Graeme Dott.

□ The players who signed are Stephen Hendry, Ronnie O'sullivan, Judd Trump, John Higgins, Neil Alexander Robertson, Stephen Lee, Markus Campbell, Mark Williams,Mark Allen, Shaun Murphy, Allister Carter, Stephen Maguire, Martin Gould, Ricky Walden, Fergal O'Brien, Stuart Bingham and Dominic Dale.

□ The Masters was the official ranking of the World Snooker Vocational Tour in Shanghai in 2007. It is also known as the World Three Competitions together with the World Championship and the UK Championship. The Shanghai Masters, known as the first brand of overseas events by the World Professional Billiards & Snooker Association (WPBSA), is one of the longest and most influential top Snooker events held in China. In 2013, Ding Junhui won the championship.

尺寸 /Size:

斯诺克球 /Snooker ball:

Φ57mm

数量 /Amount:

一套 22 枚 /Set of 22 pieces

斯诺克球杆 /Snooker pool cue:

Φ30mm × 1 600mm

年代 /Date:

当代 /Contemporary

木质网球拍

Wooden Tennis Rackets

□ 这对网球拍为民国时期的木质球拍，由拍头、拍喉、拍柄组成，以温菲尔德设计的网球拍为基础，在拍柄上施以彩绘，网线保存完好。

□ 现代网球运动诞生于 19 世纪的英国伯明翰，最初被称为“草地网球”。网球拍制作材料最初为木头，由于木质球拍重量大、刚性不够、易受潮的缺点，在 20 世纪中后期逐渐被金属球拍取代。

□ The pair of wooden tennis rackets date back to the period of the Republic of China. Based on the racket designed by Wingfield, this pair of rackets are composed of racket head, throat and handle on which there is still painting. The strings are still well preserved.

□ Modern tennis originated from Birmingham in the 19th century when it was called “Lawn Tennis”. Tennis rackets were preliminarily made by wood, but later replaced by metal since 1950s as wooden rackets are relatively heavy and susceptible to moisture with insufficient rigidity.

尺寸 /Size:
240mm × 560mm × 16mm
数量 /Amount:
2
年代 /Date:
近代 /Modern times

网球大师杯赛纪念杯

Commemorative Trophy of Tennis Masters Cup

□ 纪念杯上写有“2002 年网球大师杯赛”“上海”的英文字样，由组委会送予每位参赛选手。

□ 网球大师杯赛始于 1999 年，是男子网球巡回赛的总决赛。大师杯赛汇集了世界排名前八的网坛顶尖选手，代表了网坛最高水准的较量。2009 年开始，赛事改名为 ATP 世界巡回赛总决赛。

□ 2002 年，上海承办了本届网球大师杯赛，网坛“八大天王”莱顿・休伊特、安德烈・阿加西、马拉特・萨芬、胡安・卡洛斯・费雷罗、卡洛斯・莫亚、罗杰・费德勒、阿尔伯特・科斯塔聚首上海滩，为中国观众奉献了一场惊心动魄的争夺战，最终“澳洲野兔”休伊特成功卫冕。

□ The memorial cup is engraved with the English words “2002 Shanghai Tennis Masters Cup” and is awarded to each contestant by the Organizing Committee.

□ The Tennis Masters Cup began in 1999 as the finals of the Men's Tennis Tour. The Masters Cup brings together the top eight tennis players in the world and represents the highest level of competition in tennis. Beginning in 2009, the event was renamed the ATP World Tour Finals.

□ In 2002, the “Eight Kings” of tennis, namely Lleyton Hewitt, Andre Agassi, Marat Safin, Juan Carlos Ferrero, Carlos Moya, Roger Federer and Albert Costa, gathered in Shanghai and presented an exciting event for Chinese audiences. Finally, Hewitt, with the nickname of “Australian Hare”, defended the championship.

尺寸 /Size：
140mm × 135mm × 260mm
重量 /Weight：
4 056.4g
年代 /Date：
2002

科威特
国家男子足球队
交流礼品银壶

Silver pot presented by Kuwait National Men's Football Team

□ 银壶是一种名为"Dallah"的阿拉伯咖啡壶，壶身、壶柄和壶嘴呈弧线形设计，壶嘴大而细长，壶腹与壶盖上皆刻有花朵浮雕。整把银壶造型优美，地域文化特色鲜明，一般流行于阿拉伯半岛地区。

□ 科威特国家男子足球队成立于 1952 年，1976 年获亚洲杯亚军。1978 年，科威特足球队访问上海时赠送银壶给上海市体委。

□ the silver pot is an Arab coffee pot named "Dallah". The body, handle and spout of the pot are of arc-shaped design. The spout is large and slender. There are embossed flowers on the main part and the lid of the pot. The whole silver pot is beautiful in shape, with distinct regional and cultural characteristics. It is generally popular in the Arabian Peninsula.

□ The Kuwait National Men's Football Team was founded in 1952 and won the second prize of the AFC Asian Cup in 1976. In 1978, the Kuwait Football Team donated it to the Shanghai Sports Commission when they visited Shanghai.

尺寸 /Size:
245mm × 120mm × 240mm
重量 /Weight:
322.3g
年代 /Date:
1978

大松博文袖扣

Cufflinks of Daimatsu Hirobumi

☐ 这是 1964 年大松博文在东京奥运会上使用的袖扣。袖扣金色包边，中间以抽象的线条和点结合成一位运动员打排球的形象。

☐ 大松博文（1921—1978），日本排球界的传奇人物，创造了女排领域一个成熟的亚洲打法，使日本女排先后在 1962 年世界杯排球赛和 1964 年奥运会排球赛中获冠军，并创造了排球运动史上连胜 175 场的奇迹。

☐ These are the cuffinks that Daimatsu Hirobumi used at the Tokyo Olympics in 1964. The cufflinks are golden-cuffed, with abstract lines and dots in the middle combined to form the image of an athlete playing volleyball.

☐ Daimatsu Hirobumi (1921-1978), a legendary figure in Japanese volleyball, created a mature Asian play in the field of female volleyball, which enabled the Japanese female volleyball to win the championship in the 1962 FIVB World Cup and the 1964 Olympic Game of volleyball match and created a miracle of winning 175 consecutive games.

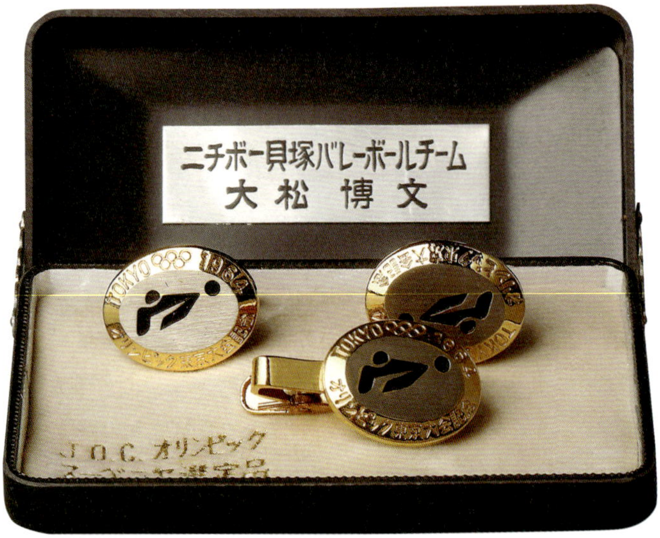

尺寸 /Size：
92mm × 62mm × 24mm
数量 /Amount：
一组 3 枚 /A set of 3
重量 /Weight：
8.8g
年代 /Date：
1964

第四展厅

EXHIBITION HALL IV

未来之窗

A WINDOW OF THE FUTURE

第四展厅

EXHIBITION HALL IV

中国特色社会主义进入新时代，
体育作为人民日益增长的
美好生活需要的
组成部分，
已经成为不可或缺的
现代生活方式和
经济社会发展的重要支撑。
上海体育站在新时代的起点上，
肩负着建设全球著名体育城市和
健康上海的任务，
以昂首挺进之姿，
奔向前所未有之境。

As socialism with Chinese
characteristics has entered
a new era,
as an integral part of
the people's growing needs for
a better life,
sports have become an indispensable
modern lifestyle and
an important support for
economic and
social development.
At the starting point of the new era,
with the task of building
a world-renowned sports city and
a healthy Shanghai,
Shanghai sports
will continue to
forge ahead to achieve
unprecedented development.

上海市
Shanghai

沉浸式沙盘

Immersive Sand Table

□ 这是位于第四展厅的沉浸式沙盘，采用三维投影的技术，达到仿裸眼 3D 的效果，并配以音效，使观众投入其中。沙盘主要展示上海在“十四五”时期所要构建形成的“四极、三片、两带、一环、多点”的公共体育设施格局。

□ “四极”，即徐家汇体育公园、虹口足球场、市民体育公园、东方体育中心；“三片”，即环淀山湖片区、环滴水湖片区、崇明陈家镇片区；“两带”，即结合“一江一河”建设，打造黄浦江滨江、苏州河滨河体育生活秀带；“一环”即外环绿带；“多点”，即包括源深体育中心、江湾体育场、市体育宫、上海国际体操中心、临港奉贤足球训练基地等在内的各级各类公共体育场馆设施。沙盘通过地图、场地照片、规划图等组成的视频展现上海在加速构建公共体育设施布局上的成就以及为加速打造国际体育赛事之都作出的努力。

□ This is an immersive sandbox in Hall 4, which employs three-dimensional projection technology to achieve a 3D imitation of the naked eye, with sound effects to keep the audience engaged. The sandbox mainly displays the “four poles, three areas, two zones, one ring and multiple points” pattern of public facilities to be formed in Shanghai in the 14th Five-Year Plan period.

□ “Four poles” include Xujiahui Sports Park, Hongkou Football Stadium, Citizen’s Sports Park, and Oriental Sports Centre; “Three areas” include Ring Dianshan Lake area, Ring Dishui Lake area, and Chongming Chenjia Town area; “Two zones” involve the construction of the “one river, one river”, to create Huangpu River riverside, Suzhou River riverside sports life area. “One ring” is the outer green belt; “multiple points” includes the Yuanshen Sports Centre, the Jiangwan Stadium, the Municipal Sports Palace, the Shanghai Garden Gymnastics Centre, and the Lingang Fengxian Football Training Base; It comprise all levels of public sports facilities. The sandbox demonstrates the achievements of Shanghai in accelerating the layout of public sports facilities and the efforts made to establish an international sporting event capital through maps, photos of venues, and planning maps.

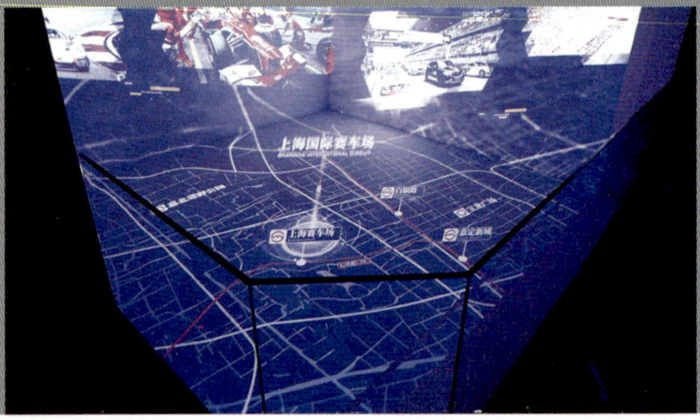

智能查询大屏

Large Intelligent Enquiry Screen

□ 这是位于第四展厅的查询大屏，可支持多人同时搜索，通过大屏，不仅可查询博物馆里的每一件展品，了解体育的相关知识，还可查询市区两级体育场馆设施建设的信息。此外，切换大屏屏幕，还可查询全市的体育设施管理服务平台，平台上数据实时更新，体现上海体育一网通办、一网统管的成果。

□ This is the large enquiry screen located in Hall 4, which can support multiple searchers at the same time. Through the large screen, it is possible to check not only every exhibit in the museum and learn about sports, but also information on the construction of sports facilities at both urban and city levels. In addition, by switching between the large screens, visitors can also check the city's sports facilities management service platform, and the data on the platform is updated in real-time, reflecting the results of Shanghai's Sports One Network and the unified management by the network.

临展：百年赛艇文化展

Temporary Exhibition: Centennial Rowing Culture Exhibition

第四展厅

EXHIBITION HALL IV

□ 上海，依水而生，因水而兴。逶迤的长江从此东流入海，古老的文明在此同世界交汇。现代赛艇运动亦从大洋彼岸乘波而来，成为最早传入上海的近代体育项目之一。

□ 从浦江上最初出现的竞渡身影起，赛艇运动已在申城悄然走过了百余年历程。百余年间，中国大地发生了天翻地覆的变化，上海始终牢牢占据着时代变革的潮头。争先竞进、乘风破浪的赛艇运动彰显着追求卓越的城市精神，在一代代赛艇健儿的接力奋进中，划进新的时代，迎来梦圆时刻。

□ Shanghai is a city born upon water and flourished in response to it. The Yangtze River flows eastwards into the sea, where ancient civilizations have met the world. The modern sport of rowing also came from across the ocean, becoming one of the first modern sports to be introduced to Shanghai.

□ Since the first sightings of rowing on the Huangpu River, rowing has quietly made its way through the city of Shanghai for over hundred years. Throughout these hundred years, China has changed dramatically, and Shanghai has consistently held the tide of the changes of the times. Rowing has been a major part of the city's spirit of excellence, with generations of rowers rowing into a new era and a dream come true.

时间 / Time：
2021.9.11–2021.10.25

荣誉证书

荣誉证书

临展：覆冰踏雪 相约冬奥

Temporary Exhibition: Covering Ice and Stepping on Snow

第四展厅

EXHIBITION HALL IV

☐ 冰雪运动，中国古已有之。隋唐时期就有记载，北方地区的人们“乘木马驰冰上，以板籍足，屈木支腋，蹴辗百步，势迅激”。至清代，已演变出统称“冰嬉”的多种竞技和游戏活动。在世界范围，近代冰雪运动发展更加成熟而广泛。全球冰雪运动的盛会——冬季奥林匹克运动会的成功举办，推动了近代冰雪运动日益走向全球化和规范化。2022 年，冬奥会和冬残奥会来到中国北京。办好这场盛会是党和国家的一件大事，是中国对国际社会的庄严承诺。中国，将为世界奉献一届精彩、非凡、卓越的奥运盛会。让我们一起享受冰雪之乐、相约北京冬奥！

☐ Ice and snow sports have been played in China since ancient times. According to records from the Sui and Tang dynasties, people in northern China “rode on wooden horses along the ice, with their feet on boards and their armpits on bent woods, the speed of the ride is a hundred paces”. Since the Qing Dynasty, there has been an evolution of a wide range of athletic and gaming activities collectively known as “ice frolics”. Around the world, ice and snow sports have become more sophisticated and widespread in modern times. The successful holding of the Winter Olympic Games, the grand event of global ice and snow sports, has promoted the increasing globalization and standardization of modern ice and snow sports. In 2022, the Winter Olympic and Paralympic will be held in Beijing, China. Hosting the Games is a major event for the Party and the country, representing a solemn commitment by China to the international community. China will provide the world with wonderful, extraordinary and outstanding Olympic Games. Let's enjoy the fun of snow and ice and meet in Beijing for the Winter Olympic!

时间 /Time：
2021.11.15–2022.10.31

高山滑雪
Alpine Skiing
跳台滑雪
Ski Jumping
速度滑冰
Speed Skating

COMPETING FOR GLORIES
ON ICE AND SNOW
逐鹿冰雪
赛场峥嵘
历届冬季奥林匹克运动会 举办时间和城市
历届冬季奥运会
参与者奖章
Successive winter Olympics
NORTH AMERICA
EUROPE
ASIA
AFRICA
SOUTH AMERICA
OCEANIA
CORTINA
1956
Offizieller
Bericht
der
IX.Olympischen
Winterspiele
Innsbruck
1964
GRENOBLE 1968
1972

上海
体育博物馆
珍品典藏

TREASURE COLLECTION
OF SHANGHAI
SPORTS MUSEUM

图书在版编目（CIP）数据

上海体育博物馆珍品典藏 / 上海市体育宣传教育中心编.
-- 上海：上海科学技术出版社, 2023.1
ISBN 978-7-5478-5915-5

Ⅰ. ①上… Ⅱ. ①上… Ⅲ. ①体育 – 博物馆 – 历史文物 – 介绍 – 上海 Ⅳ. ①K875.9

中国版本图书馆CIP数据核字(2022)第186744号

责任编辑：陈晨
书籍设计：张国樑　董伟
英文翻译：卢文斌
排版：严志强

上海体育博物馆珍品典藏
上海市体育宣传教育中心 编

上海世纪出版（集团）有限公司
上　海　科　学　技　术　出　版　社　出版、发行
（上海市闵行区号景路159弄A座9F-10F
邮政编码 201101　www.sstp.cn）
上海雅昌艺术印刷有限公司印刷
开本：787 × 1092　1/16　印张：21.5
插页：20　字数：300千字
2023年1月第1版　2023年1月第1次印刷
ISBN 978-7-5478-5915-5/G · 1123
定价：390.00元